Autographed, Limited, Commemorative Edition

(Limited to Five Thousand)

Number 163 /5000

Mattie Mullins

Mattie Carroll Mullins

Judy

The Murder of My Daughter
The Healing of My Family

by
Mattie Carroll Mullins

RECOVERY COMMUNICATIONS, INC.
P.O. Box 19910, Baltimore, Maryland 21211 • (410) 243-8558

Dedication

To Judy's sons
Forrest and Hunter
her pride and joy
who have brought happiness
beyond measure to our lives

Table of Contents

71 ILLUSTRATIONS

83 PART TWO

Foreword

DR. JOE R. STACKER
PASTOR, BELMONT HEIGHTS BAPTIST CHURCH
NASHVILLE, TENNESSEE

❧ The recovery after a death is difficult. As a pastor, I have been placed in situations of support to those in need of such recovery. I assumed this was the situation on September 7, 1994, when the phone rang and my brother-in-law, Bill Bristow, told me that Judy Mullins Freels had died in Johnson City, Tennessee. However, this time it was different. No one in our family had ever been murdered.

My wife's brother and sister-in-law, Kelver and Mattie Mullins, had experienced what most of us consider an event that happens to other people. With all my pastoral experience, I had nothing to fall back on. And if I felt the way I did, I could imagine what difficulties Kelver and Mattie were facing. How does a person recover from such a blow? How indeed, especially when all the facts were finally known?

I saw a close family come closer together in love and support. Prayers, calls, letters, cards, visits, and the presence of family and friends began the recovery even before the funeral. I doubt that recovery is possible in isolation. There are so many words that need to be spoken, and feelings shared, which one cannot do alone. That is one more reason God gave us family and friends. When I question God, or have misplaced my faith, often He is there in a loved one or friend. The touch of a grandchild, or a voice on "long distance" can bring God close, and we know we are not forgotten.

Mattie Carroll Mullins shares her story with us in the hope that it will comfort and encourage us, should we experience pain such as she and Kelver know. She found in time the presence, provision, and promise of God in Christ, as she perceived the light, even in the valley of the shadow of death. All the family had, in some way, to deal with the dynamics of Judy's death. We found it in our faith. The road has not been easy, but should one be forced to travel such a road of pain and hurt, let us do it in God's love through Jesus Christ. God is in the healing business. That is what Mattie and Kelver found.

Introduction

ATTORNEY GENERAL DAVID CROCKETT
FIRST JUDICIAL DISTRICT OF TENNESSEE

🙠 Autumn was in the air and the evenings were already getting cooler when Judy Mullins Freels answered the door at her parents' home in the early hours of September 7, 1994.

She found her husband's roommate and friend standing on the walk and stepped outside to speak with him. The man told her he had experienced car trouble and needed to borrow a jack. She asked him to wait a moment for her to open the trunk of her car. That was typical of Judy. She was a good Samaritan — her friends knew her to be a committed, devoted Christian whose actions were as generous as her words.

Judy's kind offer to help was her final one, for death claimed her there, a death more horrendous and devastating than any other in my recollection. I have been a prosecutor for nearly thirty years, and I have stood over the lifeless bodies of more victims than I care to remember. The shadow of death has darkened my own life as well. More than a decade ago — it sometimes seems like a few hours — my teenage son died in an automobile accident.

Even so, I find it hard to imagine the horror that took place at the Mullins home. That home had sheltered four children as they made good names for themselves in school, excelling in everything they did, to become honorable adults. When they were in high school, their young friends would gather regularly at the Mullins house, where hospitality was overflowing and good character was taught by example.

After Judy's death, the Mullins family proved for all the world to see that faith is the foundation for their lives. I know that it has been the rock on which they have rested as they weathered a dreadful storm.

This is a story of a family's love, faith, tragedy, and survival. As a prosecutor who worked to solve the case along with the police and criminal investigators, I came to see the true meaning of Christian strength and compassion through the Mullins family.

Judy tells the story of a rich, wonderful life that was so well lived. I consider it an honor to recommend this uplifting story to anyone and to salute the noble family who lived it.

Prologue

Wedding Vows

The date was August 15, 1987, the occasion our youngest daughter Judy's wedding.

The words spoken then will echo in my memory forever.

"I, Russell, take you, Judy, to be my wedded wife, to have and to hold, from this day forward, for better, for worse, for richer, for poorer, in sickness and in health, to love and to cherish, till death do us part, according to God's holy ordinance; and thereto I pledge you my love."

"I, Judy, take you, Russell, to be my wedded husband, to have and to hold, from this day forward, for better, for worse, for richer, for poorer, in sickness and in health, to love and to cherish, till death do us part, according to God's holy ordinance; and thereto I pledge you my love."

One special sentence the minister — Judy's father — spoke on that happy day just before the couple exchanged wedding rings stands out starkly in my mind: *"This circle may be broken honorably in the sight of God only by death."*

How little we then knew how terribly, how dishonorably that circle would break.

" . . . . I now pronounce you husband and wife. What God has joined together let no man put asunder."

Excerpt from an interview with Johnson City, Tennessee, Police Department investigators, September 7, 1994:

It's been the biggest problem in my relation with Judy for years.

She was raised a Southern Baptist and a devout non-drinker, and her family is the same way.

I've just always been a drinker, and it's probably the biggest reason we separated.

— Russell Freels

Part One

A Parent's Worst Nightmare

❧ If you were a happy wife and mother of a wonderful family of children and grandchildren, you would have every right to be grateful for such blessings. That's how my life was, until September 7, 1994. My most frightening fantasies contained nothing so horrible as the reality my husband and I had to confront in the dawning hours of that dreadful day.

Around 3:30 A.M., my three-year-old grandson, who was then living with his mother — our daughter Judy — and eight-month-old brother in our downstairs apartment, came to our bedroom crying. "MeMe, my mommy's dead. She's outside."

All children have bad dreams, I told myself, *and sometimes they walk in their sleep.*

"Forrest, go back downstairs," I told him gently. "It's too soon to get up."

"MeMe, a monster came and got my mommy."

"Forrest, now go get back in bed and go to sleep."

"A car ran over my mommy and killed her," he said.

"Honey, it's the middle of the night. Your mommy's asleep, and you need to go to sleep too."

The child spoke quietly and calmly, with a strange certainty in his voice. "MeMe, it's raining outside, and my mommy is melting."

Just then my husband Kelver woke up, and Forrest asked to get into our bed, something he had never done before. I pulled my little grandson in with us — the line of least resistance at that point.

As my husband went back to sleep, Forrest laughed. "Papaw's snoring, isn't he?"

"Yes, Forrest, he is."

I began to rub Forrest's back, and he soon fell asleep too.

About an hour later Forrest woke again, asking to go downstairs and get into his own bed. I got up and watched him go down the stairs, but at the bottom he turned back, complaining that his mother wasn't there.

I went down to look, with Forrest calling loudly: "Mommy! Mommy!"

Baby Hunter woke up crying. I picked him up and went back upstairs with both of them, turning on lights, going through the house searching for Judy. The last room was our living room, and no one was there.

The words Forrest had spoken earlier came back to me: "My mommy's dead. She's outside." It couldn't be true!

I woke Kelver. "I can't find Judy," I said.

He sat up, instantly awake. "What do you mean, you can't find Judy?"

"Forrest said she was outside."

He got up at once and pulled on his clothes, and he and I took Forrest and the baby back downstairs. As Kelver went out to investigate, I put the children on Judy's bed. "Stay there," I told them, intending to follow their grandfather outside.

But at that moment Kelver staggered back in, his face ashen. "Call 911!" he cried, making a slashing motion across his neck, then collapsing. "I think she's dead," he groaned, gasping for breath.

What else could I do? I managed to dial 911, asking with quaking voice for help to be sent, then praying aloud: "O God, help us!"

In a way that I still cannot explain, I felt strength flow through my body — strength that empowered me to go outside to see for myself this unspeakable thing.

There, in the driveway beside our basement door, I stared down at a mother's worst nightmare — my youngest child's outstretched, lifeless body. Her feet bare, fully clothed in pajamas and a robe, she lay in a pool of her own blood. Her throat had been slashed, and a stream of blood trickled down the drive. I saw other stab wounds on her body, but her beautiful face was unharmed, her gorgeous red hair untouched. She lay there as white and still as a statue, her lips forever fixed in a radiant smile.

Kelver had so far recovered himself that he was able to bring out a sleeping bag to cover her body. After he spread it over Judy, I pulled it away from her face, in the vain hope that she might possibly still be alive.

Dear God, what evil could have brought such a tragedy upon us? How would we ever endure such agonizing pain?

A Close Family, A True Home

❧   Our hilltop home was a comfortable ranch-style house, its welcoming front porch hung with flowering plants. We had lived there for nearly thirty years, during most of my husband Kelver's service in ministry. Our children had grown up there — a boy and three girls. Very few families, particularly preachers' families, are privileged to remain so long in one place. We cherished the stability that had been ours during all those years.

Johnson City, our pleasant East Tennessee home, had grown since our coming from a small community where everyone knew everyone else, to a university city with an influx of professional people, new enterprises, and recent retirees. Yet it is still a close-knit community in many ways. We are deeply grateful that our town, like many other good places, is one in which people care about one another, help one another, and respond generously to human need.

A Life Centered in Faith, Education, and Family

❧   Our family life has always revolved around the church. I had grown up in a Christ-centered home in Bluefield, West Virginia, following my three brothers to Baptist-supported Carson-Newman College in Jefferson City, Tennessee. My future husband Kelver was also a student there, and during a freshman talent show someone pointed me out onstage, where I was playing the ukelele and singing, telling Kelver, "Right there is a girl you ought to date."

"That'll be the last girl on this campus I'll ever date!" he responded. Well, I was!

After both of us graduated, we married and moved to Texas so that Kelver could enroll at Southwestern Baptist Theological Seminary to study religious education, while I worked full-time and attended some classes. After his master's degree was awarded, we moved back to East Tennessee where Kelver became educational director at a church in Morristown, going on later to a similar position in Chattanooga. Our first child, Andrew Carroll ("Andy"), was born while we lived there.

Eventually, sensing God's call to the ordained ministry, Kelver resigned his position and moved us to Johnson City, where he was ordained and took up a pastorate at Bethel Baptist Church. During his ministry there, he continued attending graduate school at East Tennessee State University, earning a second master's degree. Faith, family love, and education have always been the stars our family has steered by.

After Andy's birth I had given up my schoolteaching position, perfectly satisfied to be "just" a minister's wife, mother, homemaker, Sunday-School teacher, church pianist and organist, and active in our local home demonstration club. As Sanda Elaine, Rebecca Jane, and finally Judith Charmane came along to complete our little brood, it was my great joy to be a caregiver and daily participant in their young lives.

Kelver and I were very proud of all our children, but after Judy arrived, she soon became the special joy of our entire clan. Little Sanda was only three when Judy was born, Becky just thirteen months old. We brought tiny, red-haired Judy home from the hospital, and when two neighbors came to call, Mother's little helper Sanda answered their knock.

"Hello, Sanda," they said happily. "We've come to see the baby!"

"Which baby?" Sanda asked in confusion. "The old one or the new one?"

After "baby" Judy reached kindergarten age, the Johnson City schools were in desperate need of substitute teachers, and I was asked to help. With our three older children already in school, I registered Judy for a morning kindergarten and enlisted my sister-in-law to keep her in the afternoons. The school principal soon asked me to take a permanent teaching spot, so I became a working mom again. I enjoyed getting back into the teaching world, and to my great satisfaction, Judy soon came to feel that she had two homes — her home with Kelver and me and her sisters and brother, and her home with her Uncle Raiford and Aunt Katherine. For all thirty-one of Judy's precious years on earth, she remained extremely close to these dear kin.

A PICTURE-BOOK FAMILY

❧   A special member of our household was our beautiful tan Collie dog, Misty. Every morning Misty would escort our four children down our steep driveway and stand at the edge of the road until the school bus stopped and its door opened. After Judy, Becky, Sanda, and Andy climbed aboard, Misty would turn and plod back up the hill, satisfied that the children were safely inside. She could always hear the bus coming long before any of the rest of us and would repeat her downhill journey in the afternoons to greet the children as they returned home.

A happy loving family, a comfortable home, even a faithful family dog — we could have asked for nothing more. We felt humbly but richly blessed.

A Girl Who Made Things Happen

ﺰ﮲ After Judy entered elementary school, she quickly demonstrated her ambition and enthusiasm. For a recycling contest, she and a friend collected more than a ton of newspapers to win second place. In middle school, she was a standout in volleyball. She received a White House Award of Excellence from President Richard Nixon, for "outstanding achievement in environmental protection services." From her earliest days, Judy was destined to make her mark on the world.

I was Judy's first piano teacher, instilling in her a love for all types of music. She went on to study organ as well and learned to play the vibraharp, clarinet, and handbells. She loved to sing — solos, duets, trios, and in various choirs.

In connection with the strong faith that undergirded her entire life, Judy wrote in her scrapbook of her conversion experience:

> *At the age of twelve, I was asked by my mother if I had ever thought about accepting Christ as my Savior. Then it dawned on me what life was really like. I talked to my dad asking questions. He very patiently explained to me the plan of salvation. He encouraged me to ask Jesus into my life. The next day, I walked down the aisle at church. It was very special when my dad baptized me.*

In high school, Judy participated joyously in the choir and served as music librarian, being honored as the outstanding music student of the year. She played clarinet in the band, served on the yearbook staff, and was active in the Bible Club, while continuing her piano and organ studies. Judy's teen life was full and worthwhile. Today we cherish the numerous trophies and plaques she received for her accomplishments, preserving them to hand on to her sons when they grow up.

During those same years Judy became a member of Acteens, the Southern Baptist missions organization for teenage girls. The Acteens program included Bible study, missions education, trips to nursing homes, Mothers' Day observances, making tray favors for hospital patients, and activities for senior citizens. Judy participated eagerly. She was the daughter any parent would be thrilled to have. Looking back over Judy's scrapbook, I believe some words from the Acteen song "This is Our Day" epitomize everything our girl stood for:

> *Our God has put us here,*
> *Sharing His love,*
> *Making His message clear* . . . .

Her scrapbook included personal letters from foreign missionaries whom Judy and her sister Becky had written to and prayed for. Through Acteens, the two sisters completed the required rigorous preparation and were then commissioned to go, at their own expense, to Pippa Passes, Kentucky, an Appalachian mission center, for eight wonderful days.

Judy loved the Christian summer camp she and Becky attended, being particularly struck by the testimonies of the missionaries they heard speak. Clearly, Judy was leaning toward a life of full-time Christian outreach and service.

A YOUNG WOMAN WHO LIVED HER FAITH

≀❧　When we began sorting out Judy's belongings after her death, I discovered that she had several Bibles in her possession. One was a personalized Bible that Kelver and I had presented to her and Russell when they married, for use in their home. Today it is another keepsake we have put away for their two sons. Because Judy had more than one Bible, we have been able to save one for each of her children and share the others with special interested family members and friends. Reading from Judy's worn study Bible has been a great source of strength to me. Many verses are underlined, and her marginal notes highlight the strong truths of God's Word. A passage Judy particularly loved is Philippians 4:4-7:

Rejoice in the Lord always; again I will say rejoice. Let all men know your forbearance. The Lord is at hand. Have no anxiety about anything, but in everything by prayer and supplication with thanksgiving let your requests be made known unto God. And the peace of God, which passes all understanding, will keep your hearts and your minds in Christ Jesus.

On the back flyleaf of this Bible, Judy had also written these words from the poet Tagore: *"Death is not extinguishing the light. It is putting out the lamp because the dawn has come."* After such a sudden and shocking end to Judy's life, we find it a great comfort to know that our precious daughter thought of death in that beautiful way.

ACTS OF LOVE AND CARING

One Acteens opportunity was the "adoption" of a shut-in or invalid as a special friend. Judy chose an elderly lady named Mrs. Ward from a retirement center near our home whose only daughter was a missionary in South America. Thereafter, each week Judy planned something special — a phone call, a pretty card (frequently made from "scratch"), and occasionally a homemade goodie from our kitchen — and saw to it that Mrs. Ward's personal needs from the grocery or drugstore were bought and delivered to her. On Mother's Day, Judy sent her a delicate orchid corsage — a remembrance that meant everything to this lady whose only child was half a world away.

Judy had been prepared to report on her friendship with Mrs. Ward in a special recognition service at church, at a time when Mrs. Ward was in the hospital recuperating from surgery. Just before the service, Mrs. Ward suddenly died. In spite of her grief, Judy insisted on going ahead with her report, concluding tearfully: "This morning God called Mrs. Ward to Heaven. I am so thankful she was mine for this year."

Even after Judy was married and had small children, she gave a day each week to deliver Meals on Wheels. Judy became extremely close to the recipients, often attending to their other personal needs and wishes. Once she went back to a diabetic man's trailer to take him

29

sugar-free Jell-O, because he was unable to get out to a grocery store and craved something sweet and good.

Shortly before Judy's death, an elderly lady said to her, "These meals are real good, but why don't they ever send cornbread and beans?" Any Southerner will understand that plaintive request! To us, beans and cornbread are the food of comfort, the essential food of life. The next Saturday, when meals were not delivered, Judy cooked a potful of pinto beans and a pan of cornbread and delivered them, along with pickled beets, homemade chow-chow relish, and sweet onions, to the joy of the lady whose dinner they became.

During all those teen years while many girls were preoccupied with clothing, hair-dos, boyfriends, and talking on the telephone, Judy was thinking earnestly how to live out her faith, doing loving things for others, seeking in every way to grow and become a better person — not for personal glory, but for the joy of serving her fellow human beings and her Lord.

THE COLLEGE YEARS

꙳ After high school Judy followed her brother and sisters to Carson-Newman. Kelver and I joked that our tuition payments must have bought at least one building on that campus! The closeness between Becky and Judy was so remarkable that they chose to be college roommates — something rarely seen between sisters.

Judy excelled academically and in other ways. She was the first female president of the Ministerial Association and chairman of the Baptist Student Union Outreach Program. She chose a major in Religion and a minor in Psychology, wanting to forge an ever-stronger foundation for her faith and a deeper understanding of those she would serve in years to come.

Her musical interests also endured. She traveled with the Seed Company, a student ensemble that sang in churches throughout the region. When we first heard the beautiful solo Judy always sang on Seed Company programs, "To Know the Heart of Jesus," we were deeply touched. We could not have known that just a few years later we would be listening sorrowfully to her recorded voice singing it the night before we laid her body to rest.

Like other students, Judy found summer jobs, one of them in Sevierville, a vacation destination just outside Great Smoky Mountains National Park. There she worked in a store owned by Lois Starkey, who became Judy's good friend. When the store stayed open late, Judy would often spend the night at the Starkeys' house rather than driving home on dark mountainous roads.

"She was a very warm, outgoing person, always willing to help somebody, " Lois Starkey told a reporter for Sevierville's *Mountain Press* after Judy's shocking murder was announced. "She was like part of the family." Like so many other good folks, the Starkey family was stunned and horrified by Judy's death. "She was such a strong person, personality-wise. She was a little tiny person, a little tiny red-headed girl, about five feet tall. She was just precious. This is so terrible," Mrs. Starkey mourned. Terrible, indeed.

During those college years, Judy also volunteered for a summer mission program in Ohio, where she led Vacation Bible Schools, Backyard Bible Clubs, and Bible study, taught crafts, and carried out visitations. She found this another wonderfully rewarding and fulfilling experience. Clearly, Judy's call to Christian service was being reinforced day by day.

At some point during her college days, Judy made the acquaintance of a young man named Russell Freels — an acquaintance that did not seem significant at the time.

LIFE IN THE BIG WORLD

❧   After graduation Judy took a job in Gatlinburg, managing a discount store where Lois Starkey ran into her again, as she later remarked to the reporter from the *Mountain Press*. "I told her my daughter Beth needed a job, and Judy said, 'Send her down here and I'll put her to work.' That was so typical of Judy, that she would do what she could to help a friend."

Eventually Judy decided to return home to work for a large retail chain. She was corresponding at the time with Southwestern Baptist Seminary — her father's alma mater — hoping to do graduate work. We told Judy we would support her move to Texas if that was her decision.

A ROMANCE UNFOLDS

ᘒ   But then suddenly everything changed. While Judy was still living at home, a call came from that casual acquaintance — Russell Freels. He wanted to come to see her. Judy was ecstatic. She searched for and found a picture of him to show us and could not say enough good about him. We were happy to have him in our home as a guest.

And so Russell came, and he and Judy went out for an evening together that Judy described as "delightful." Before long he was coming repeatedly. It soon became quite clear which way the relationship was tending. Judy accepted a transfer with her company to a store that was closer to Russell, and as the months passed, their relationship blossomed into a full-blown romance. Eventually a jubilant Judy phoned asking her dad and me to come to Knoxville to meet the two of them and Russell's parents. When Judy told us she intended to marry Russell, her father asked one question: "Are you in love again?"

Judy's smiling answer came: "Not 'again.' I have never felt this way about a person before."

As we four parents listened, Judy and Russell told us they loved one another, asked for our approval, and said they very much wanted our help and participation in planning their wedding. What more could we say?

In the months that followed we had some concerns, but we considered that they were Judy's to handle, not ours. Russell's family belonged to a different denomination from ours — nothing wrong with that, but our family was thoroughly steeped in the Baptist tradition, around which most of Judy's young life had been centered. We trusted Russell and Judy to work matters out in their own way.

Judy had always hoped to become a missionary, or a missionary's or pastor's wife, or the wife of someone on a church staff, yet Russell had no idea of pursuing any such vocation. Again, we knew that this must be her choice. We could only pray that she was making the best decision for a life's mate.

Russell's talents included art, and Judy showed us a landscape he had painted as her engagement gift. On the back was written, "If ever in your life you need a friend, I'll be right here for you. Russ."

It was obvious that Russell's parents loved, respected, and adored this beautiful girl who wanted to change her name to theirs. And why wouldn't they? Any family would be lucky to claim her.

32

Wedding Plans

ક Wedding plans became the family focus for months. Judy and Russell set the date for a candlelight evening service, and Judy took charge with her usual topnotch organizational skills. Attendants' dresses were selected, flowers, music, a caterer. Judy wanted an all-white wedding — the perfect dream of a young woman deeply in love. We did all we could to make her dream come true. Judy wanted her dad to officiate at her wedding, and she had several sessions with him working thoughtfully and carefully to plan the wedding ceremony and choose the Scriptures to be read.

Russell participated willingly in the planning, helping to choose invitations and wedding attendants, and adding his family's names to the guest list. As time went on, he became "Rusty" to us. With our large extended family, we knew we could expect a great turnout. Family occasions are very special with us, and everyone wants to be there.

As the time for the wedding drew near, parties were given by family and friends — teas, showers, a luncheon for the attendants. Excitement mounted in both households.

Typically, Judy had thought out every detail. At the rehearsal she asked the members of the wedding party whether they would be willing to read a Scripture verse during the ceremony. All hands were raised, and Judy flitted happily around handing out the cards she had prepared with a verse on each one.

Judy's sister Rebecca was her maid of honor. Her sister Sanda was matron of honor, and Judy wore Sanda's wedding gown. Judy's brother Andy would escort her down the aisle, since her father was officiating, and Andy's oldest son Zachery was pleased to serve as ring bearer. In going through her personal effects after her death, I found her handwritten diagram marking the position of each attendant at the front of the church during the service.

The Sacrament Of Marriage

ક The setting and the wedding ceremony itself were as perfect as Judy had hoped. All the flowers and church decorations were done in white — Judy's pure-white wedding. The baptistry cross was draped with white, accented with magnolia blossoms. It made a truly lovely scene.

Judy included an old wedding tradition in her plans. When Rusty took his place at the front of the church, he alone among the men in the wedding party wore no boutonniere. After Judy walked down the aisle on her brother's arm, radiant and smiling, she removed from her bouquet one perfect white rose and pinned it lovingly to her groom's lapel. It was a very touching moment.

Judy's father then began to speak those well-known and much-loved words:

"Dearly beloved, we are gathered together here in the sight of God, and in the presence of these witnesses, to join together this man and this woman in holy matrimony, which is an honorable estate, instituted of God, and signifying unto us the mystical union which exists between Christ and His church; which holy estate Christ adorned and beautified with his presence in Cana of Galilee. It is therefore not to be entered into unadvisedly, but reverently, discreetly, and in the fear of God. Into this holy estate these two persons come now to be joined.

"I would encourage you both, as you stand in the presence of God, before whom the secrets of all hearts are disclosed, that, having duly considered the holy covenant you are about to make, you do now declare before this company your pledge of faith, each to the other. Be well assured that if these solemn vows are kept inviolate, as God's Word demands, and if steadfastly you endeavor to do the will of your heavenly Father, God will bless your marriage, will grant you fulfillment in it, and will establish your home in peace.

"Russell, will you have this woman to be your wedded wife, to live together in the holy estate of matrimony? Will you love her, comfort her, honor and keep her in sickness and health; and forsaking all others keep you only unto her so long as you both shall live?"

Russell's reply: "I will."

"Judy, will you have this man to be your wedded husband, to live together in the holy estate of matrimony? Will you love him, comfort him, honor and keep him in sickness and in health; and forsaking all others keep you only unto him so long as you both shall live?"

Judy's voice was clearly audible: "I will."

Kelver then addressed Russell's parents. "Judy's mother and I are pleased to ask you to accept our daughter as your daughter, too. Thank you for the Christian values you have taught your son. We have grown to love and respect Russell, and we are pleased today to receive him into our hearts as a son."

Then, speaking again to the groom: "Russell, we are pleased to present our daughter, Judy, to be joined to you as wife during this ceremony. We believe you to be a person of Christian integrity who is seeking to follow God's will. We proudly receive you today as a son. We commit Judy to you in complete confidence that you will care for her needs and seek to make her happy in Christian love and marriage.

"Who gives this woman to be married to this man?"

Andy spoke up: "Her mother, father, and I."

THE GREATEST OF THESE IS LOVE

❧ "The Bible tells us the greatest love story ever written," Kelver declared. "The greatest lover is God who gave us His only begotten Son to die that we may live. God is Love. Paul recorded for us in First Corinthians, Chapter 13, the basis of love for our lives. Listen to these inspiring words from the Revised Standard Version of the Bible." Each of the attendants in the wedding then recited a verse of that familiar chapter:

If I speak in the tongues of men and of angels, but have not love,
I am a noisy gong or a clanging cymbal.
And if I have prophetic powers, and understand all mysteries and all
knowledge, and if I have all faith, so as to remove mountains,
but have not love, I am nothing.
If I give away all I have, and if I deliver my body to be burned, but
have not love, I gain nothing.
Love is patient and kind; love is not jealous or boastful;
It is not arrogant or rude. Love does not insist on its own way; it
is not irritable or resentful;
It does not rejoice at wrong, but rejoices in the right.
Love bears all things, believes all things, hopes all things, endures
all things.
Love never ends; as for prophecies, they will pass away; as for
tongues, they will cease; as for knowledge, it will pass away.
For our knowledge is imperfect and our prophecy is imperfect;
But when the perfect comes, the imperfect will pass away.

*When I was a child, I spoke like a child; I thought like a child,
I reasoned like a child. When I became a man, I gave up
childish ways.*

*For now we see in a mirror dimly, but then face to face. Now I know
in part; then shall I understand fully, even as I have been fully
understood.*

*So faith, hope, love abide, these three; but the greatest of these
is Love.*

After a brief pause, Kelver then turned to the groom: "Russell,
repeat after me."

*I, Russell, take you, Judy, to be my wedded wife, to have
and to hold, from this day forward, for better, for worse,
for richer, for poorer, in sickness and in health, to love
and to cherish, till death do us part, according to God's
holy ordinance; and thereto I pledge you my love.*

Russell recited the words.

"Judy, repeat after me," her father said.

*I, Judy, take you, Russell, to be my wedded husband, to
have and to hold, from this day forward, for better, for
worse, for richer, for poorer, in sickness and in health,
to love and to cherish, till death do us part, according to
God's holy ordinance; and thereto I pledge you my love.*

Judy gave her solemn pledge and commitment.

Kelver continued. "From time immemorial, the ring has been used
as a symbol of a sealed bargain and contract, a vow made between two
parties. In the long ago, it was used by kings to seal contracts made
between nations. Today, we use the wedding band in our marriage
ceremonies to symbolize a lasting promise of love and devotion, to serve
as a visible symbol of that which is never-ending in our hearts one for
the other.

"These rings are made of gold, expressing the purity which should
always be in your marriage. They are made in circles, expressing the
unending qualities of your love in the eternal love of God. This circle
may be broken honorably in the sight of God only by death.

"As a token of your vows, you will now give and receive the rings."

Russell and Judy smilingly slipped wedding bands onto one another's
finger.

"And now, having pledged your love and devotion to each other and unto God the challenge taken by both of you to love and live for the other as long as you both shall live, culminating your love in the will of God, acting by the law vested in me by this state and by the spiritual privilege from the Father, I pronounce you husband and wife. What God has joined together, let no man put asunder.

"Russell, you may kiss the bride.

"God reminds us in the Song of Solomon to:
" *'Set Him as a seal upon your heart,*
   As a seal upon your arm;
   For love is strong as death . . . .
   Many waters cannot quench love.' "

Kelver was nearing the end of the service he and Judy had so carefully planned.

"May this be your commitment to each other:
" *'For whither thou goest, I will go;*
   And where thou lodgest, I will lodge;
   Thy people shall be my people, and thy God my God.'
   Now: The Lord bless you and keep you,
      The Lord make His face to shine upon you,
      And be gracious unto you,
      The Lord lift up His countenance upon you,
      And give you peace. Amen."

Directing the bridal couple to turn and face the congregation, Kelver said with a happy smile, "I now present to you Mr. and Mrs. Russell Fredrick Freels."

A GIFT OF A BIBLE

& At Andy's and Tonya's marriage Kelver and I had started a family tradition of presenting the newlyweds with a Bible, embossed in gold with their names. The next one went to Sanda and her husband Shannon in their turn. Judy and Russell received theirs. Later, when Becky and Stephen married, a fourth Bible was designated for them.

At the conclusion of each wedding ceremony our children's dad presented the newlyweds with this special Bible, asking them to use it in their home for individual study and family devotions. Little Forrest and Hunter will one day receive Judy's presentation Bible along with their mother's other keepsakes.

All who were present on that special day felt every confidence that this marriage had been solemnized in accordance with God's will. Two families happily acknowledged a closeness as our children became one in the sanctity of the marriage bond.

We continued happily on to the wedding reception, thankful that this marriage was getting off to such a fine start. On all sides, people said Judy and Russell were "made for each other."

After the bride's and groom's cakes had been cut and preparations made for the couple's departure, Judy joyfully tossed her bouquet, then ran and kissed me, saying, "Mom, I'll never forget this day. I could only be happier in Heaven." Judy never forgot her Savior's promise, that she would live with Him eternally.

Smiling and waving, the bride and groom climbed into a friend's antique Model A roadster to be driven to the hotel before setting out the next morning for Florida and a Caribbean cruise. Judy's father and I could relax, thinking that our daughter's new life would proceed in every way as it should.

A New Household

ɤ Judy and Rusty made their first home in Sevierville, where she had previously worked and made friends. He was assistant manager at a restaurant and seemingly loved his job. She continued her retail employment. One of the first decisions they made was about church affiliation. After visiting various churches, they settled on First Baptist, and Rusty made a public rededication and asked to be baptized. Kelver and I were there on that important occasion. We assumed the marriage was happy, but we didn't know every detail of their life together.

Three years passed in seeming tranquility, and then Judy and Rusty told us they were expecting a baby — an announcement we greeted with joy. After Forrest was born on November 1, 1990, Judy soon went back to work, leaving home before daylight and delivering Forrest to the babysitter on her way. She kept up with the usual chores of homemaking and motherhood and seemed as happy as a lark, even with her challenging schedule.

A NEW ENVIRONMENT

ॐ   About a year after Forrest's birth, a major change took place when Rusty accepted a new job that sent him to our area for four months' training. We had plenty of room to offer them in our own home, and because we had brought my ailing elderly mother to live with us, I needed help in caring for her. Judy loved her grandmother dearly and was more than willing to help out. So Judy, Rusty, and fourteen-month old Forrest came to make their home with us — temporarily, as we supposed.

Through the months that followed, our little grandson was a daily joy. Judy loved reading to him and teaching him one new thing every day, repeating all the things he had learned before. He quickly learned colors, animals, and how to count. We often heard Judy call Forrest "my little man."

By now Rusty was staying away from his family for long hours, supposedly because of work, or because he had places to go and people to see. These places and people often related to sports — golfing, skiing, and sailing. We did not know his friends. He purchased costly sports equipment on credit cards — a sailboat, skis, fine new golf clubs — incurring bills that would later have to be paid. Rusty had become an habitual spender, including gifts for Judy that she neither needed nor wanted. With financial pressures piling up, Judy sought new ways to bring in income and continued her sewing, crafts, cooking, and gardening, often selling her crafts.

During Rusty's increasing absences, she filled her time with attention to elderly people, those with handicaps, and people in crisis. She wrote many cards and notes to persons she cared about and continued delivering Meals on Wheels, even after the discovery that she was expecting another child.

JOYFUL HOLIDAY PREPARATIONS

ॐ   Christmas was Judy's favorite holiday, and during her second pregnancy she kept busy crafting about 200 Santas to be hung on a special Christmas tree, which we put up for the first time a month before her baby was born. The following Christmas, after her death, I had little heart for Christmas fanfare. But knowing Judy's love for the holiday rituals, I was certain she would want us to make merry. And so, hard as

39

it was for us, we put up that tree again and decorated it with Judy's Santas. We cried a lot as we did it, but it was good to feel a part of Judy still in our midst. Every Christmas since, her Santa tree takes the prominent spot in our living room.

A NEW BABY

❧ Judy and Rusty's second son, Hunter Christian, was born January 17, 1994, in the midst of a blizzard. We were all extremely concerned when the doctors told us he was in respiratory distress and needed artificial ventilation. After it was decided to transfer him to a neonatal intensive-care unit, he had to be taken there by special ambulance over icy roads in a snowstorm. Judy was understandably in great turmoil. Complications from the delivery kept her five days in the hospital, away from her newborn son.

And at some point she had discovered that Rusty was drinking heavily and using other drugs, in company with his disturbing new friends. She kept most of this unpleasantness to herself, hoping to shield us.

She longed desperately to be with her new baby, and when Hunter was twelve days old she and Rusty were finally able to bring him home. Since then, thank goodness, he has been a very healthy child.

NEW DIRECTIONS ARE REQUIRED

❧ Judy was coming to see that she might eventually have to earn a living on her own. As soon as she was able, she took the necessary training, sat for the state test, and received a Tennessee license to write health and life insurance, becoming an associate of a well-known insurance firm. Her love for people, outgoing personality, and sales ability quickly brought clients to her. She was named Associate of the Month in the district, and company-wide awards came her way. Even today, many people tell me they continue to appreciate the benefits of policies Judy wrote.

Another new direction came when Judy accepted an invitation to attend a demonstration of a special line of kitchenware. After this fun-filled evening she returned home in great excitement and said she would love to be able to arrange these shows herself. I encouraged her to pursue this goal, knowing she would be perfect for the job and could certainly use any money brought in from sales.

Thereafter she conducted kitchen demonstrations about two nights each week. Forrest was by then two years old, and sometimes I kept him and the baby while Judy was out. At other times if Rusty had time off, he might occasionally stay around to look after the children. Judy made a name for herself with the kitchenware company, just as she did in all else she undertook.

After going along with her to demonstrations several times, I became her assistant, washing up in the kitchen and finishing a recipe she had started so that Judy could move on to the next recipe on the agenda. I look back now on those times with fond remembrance of our shared fun and the boost it gave to Judy's morale.

One of her favorite pastimes was baking cookies. Always keeping cookie dough made up in the refrigerator, at least three evenings a week she would bake a batch of chocolate chip, peanut butter, or raisin oatmeal cookies and dash out to the restaurant where Rusty worked so he could have a delectable homemade snack. One of Judy's favorite cookie recipes is reproduced in the Appendix at the end of this book.

A Tribute From Her Peers

*After Judy's death, Chris McDaneld, director of Pampered Chef in East Tennessee, dedicated the front page of the organization's newsletter to Judy.

Precious Memories

One of the things that I love so much about my job is all the wonderful people . . . . One of these . . . . was Judy Freels. Judy was a beautiful person — both inside and out. She was a professional; she was talented and compassionate. It is to the memory of this precious friend that we dedicate this month's newsletter. We will sorely miss her warm smile and sweet spirit. We share in the grief of her parents and her children as we mourn her death and the horrid circumstances surrounding it . . . .

'Give and it will be given to you, a good measure, pressed down, shaken together and running over, will be poured into

your lap. For with the measure you use it will be measured to you.' Luke 6:38.

I thank God for allowing me the privilege of knowing and working with Judy, and the world is a better place because she lived.

GATHERING CLOUDS

ớ♣ After Rusty's company transferred him to Alabama, Judy and the children remained with us as he supposedly looked for housing for his family. But after weeks and months passed, with no housing being found, we knew there was profound trouble in their marriage. Acutely aware of Judy's need for emotional support, we tried to be there for her every day. Rusty's parents also constantly offered encouragement and sympathy. They came often to visit, letting Judy know she had their moral support and showering love on their two little grandsons.

FAMILY AGONY OVER ADDICTION

ớ♣ During this period Judy told her dad and me that Rusty was drinking heavily and using other drugs. We were all deeply troubled, believing that he was associating with the wrong people, engaging in activities that were unacceptable to us and inappropriate to his role as Christian husband and father. Many people saw that the marriage was falling apart.

Judy sought help from Rusty's parents, her pastor, and others. She bought a set of videos on Marriage and the Family, as well as books dealing with alcoholism and other drugs. She read or watched them all, encouraging Rusty to do the same. Judy believed he sincerely wanted to change, and she was the soul of patience and understanding as she tried to get Rusty to accept professional counseling. She believed he was ready, and she offered to go with him. He promised he would leave the restaurant business, which she considered an undesirable environment for him, and said he would let alcohol alone and abandon other destructive influences. But none of these changes took place, and eventually an attorney was consulted. We knew that without a drastic turnaround, divorce was probably in the offing.

A LOVING UNCLE'S LETTER OF CONCERN

As I understand it now, Judy, like most relatives of people with addictive disease, was trying desperately to fix the family problems herself — something that's humanly impossible for anyone. My brother Dan Carroll came for a visit, picked up immediately on her situation, and discussed it with her. Four months before Judy's death, he wrote her a touching and compassionate letter.

My dear Judy,

I have been wanting to write to you and let you know of our love and support for you in these days. In fact, I just wish that you could drive out here with your kids for a nice, long visit with us . . . . and stay as long as you would like. Our kids think so much of you and would be thrilled if you could come. To all of us you are very special and we can feel for you with what you are going through.

Romans 8:28 is my favorite verse and is still valid in that God can take any tragedy and bring good out of it, even though that is hard to understand.

Judy, I am not able to give you any advice, but I do pledge to you my prayer support and love. Your life is so precious and I do know that God loves you more than you can imagine. Please don't ever give up. You have so much to offer with your life regardless of what you are going through. I know that you have been an inspiration to so many people with your winsome smile and positive personality. Don't forget the verse in the 23rd Psalm which says, "Yea, though I walk through the valley . . . . " The word "through" means that you will come through the valley and be able to see the other side. You will not always stay in the valley as you might think.

Judy, I have always admired you for being so smart and for your sweet spirit. I know that you are a good mother to your children. And years later they will bless you for your love and faithfulness to them. I am also going to continue to pray for Rusty. I cannot be a judge, but I feel that his problem may not be with you, Judy, but with the Lord. We are all praying that somehow he may come to full submission to the Lord's plan and will for his life.

There may be friends who have offered advice to you as to what to do in your situation, but I am not that smart. The only word of wisdom that I would suggest is that you just stay close to the Lord and not make any decisions unless you feel a definite leading by the Holy Spirit. His way is always perfect. I feel certain that He will show you answers that you need as you read His Word day by day. I pray that God's guardian angels will watch over you constantly day and night and that you can feel His presence very close to you moment by moment. Remember, Judy, that you are never alone and that His Spirit is right there with you even in your lowest moments. Please, remember that we love you and pray for you every morning in our devotional time.

> *Love in Christ,*
> *Uncle Dan*

Judy wrote a reply to this letter but for whatever reason, never mailed it. It was found, after her murder, among her papers at home.

Uncle Ran, Aunt B Alice
The words to thank you
for your kind letter — well are
hard to find. Most of
my family is angry and
judgmental of what I am
going through. You words
were thoughtful and sincere.
Thank you. Thank you.

I would be lying if I
told you I was fine. I
am torn apart and very
confused. You see for 8
yrs Rusty has been my
husband, father of my
sons, and most of all my
best friend. He means
so much to me. I ache
at the thought of losing

him. He has been so honest and kind through all of this separation. He still sends me his entire check. He calls almost daily and the wants us to remain the best of friends. I know in they heart that he loves me dearly but he doesn't want to hurt me & the boys. I know this all sounds like an immature girl who won't let go but I have been thro all of this over + over again and I know Rusty is just really in a whirl of sin and the alcohol

has control of his life.
I love & pray for him
daily. It is a love that
has worked through
2½ yrs of hiding his
faults because I that
I had to protect my
kids & my family's good
name. If I could crawl
in a whole somewhere
to save my parents
embarrassment for all
of this I would today.
Mother is especially
upset and angry with
Rusty for his unwilling-
ness to change
    I in no way want
to defend his actions

however, I respect him
not making me live
in fear and lonliness
for years to come with
an uncommitted
husband and alcoholic.
 Several months back
before Hunter was born
Rusty asked me for help —
to find him some profess-
ional help with his
problem of alcohol and
my pride and embarass-
ment and literally
my ignorance of the
disease — well, I kept
thinking it would just
go away. Now I live
everyday with the that

of what life may be today, had I admitted failure and helped him.

Rusty has never hurt me or the children in any way. He has always been the kindest loving mate I could hope to have. He simply is not ready for a daily walk with the Lord and the daily responsibilities of a family. I cherish our 8 yrs together and would love him to my death if he would let me but for now I have to somehow let him go and trust his life to God. Oh how I pray constantly for him.

The 25th Psalm has come to touch me. I am greatly ashamed for any part in this failure that I have had.

I am broken and truly in the "wilderness" for now. But that only means one day I can come out to better land. I hurt but I know God is forever w/ me and mine.

Thank you for your love and prayers. Please

know Rusty is a wonderful
man. He is just so
lost and weak now.
   Please pray for mom
+ Dad to have strength
thro this. I would
give anything to save
their + the Freels from
hurt and embarrassment.
The entire Freels clan
have rallied to my side
with support. I pray
that people will use
the angry energy for
Russell to pray for his
relationship w/ God
+ his Church.
      I love you both
         Judy

Others in our family took many opportunities to discuss the problems with Judy. Her brother Andy offered numerous suggestions that she did not take. I suppose she just couldn't grasp the seriousness or true nature of Rusty's problems. None of us really knew what she experienced, felt, or thought.

Loss Of A Grandmother

ɜ& A month before Judy was murdered, while she and I were out of town at a kitchenware convention, my mother's condition suddenly worsened, and we received the sorrowful phone call telling us she had died. We immediately returned home. At the age of 104, my mother had become so weary that she was praying every day for God to take her, and so, when her wish was finally granted, our desire for her final peace was such that none of us felt inconsolable grief.

After the funeral, with Rusty far away in Alabama, we continued adjusting to life without either him or my mother in our midst. Kelver, Judy, the little boys and I rested, relaxed, and were able to do many things that we had put on hold during the previous two years. These were four wonderful, wonderful weeks. We worked, laughed, played, and all drew closer to one another.

Even so, Judy kept a pretty structured schedule. She had to, to get in all the things she had to do. After breakfast every morning she prepared eight bottles for baby Hunter, to supply him throughout the day and night, with one bottle left for the early morning feeding.

She bought a a personal computer and updated her résumé, mailing out twenty-two copies to area businesses just two days before she was killed. Life was taking a more positive and hopeful turn. There were endings, and there were new beginnings.

Reunion Plans

ɜ& Reviving dying hopes, Rusty scheduled a September vacation with Judy and the children, intending to visit Judy's sister Becky and her family in Jacksonville, Florida. Becky's husband Stephen and Rusty had been college roommates and remained good friends. Wanting time alone with Rusty to try to work things out, Judy asked Becky if she would keep Forrest and Hunter for one night during their stay. Becky assured her that she would. Both Becky and Stephen were doing all they could to help the faltering marriage.

On Monday September 5, we had a yard sale. On Tuesday September 6, leaving Hunter with Sanda, Judy, Forrest, and I drove out to my grandparents' country homeplace, which was soon to be sold at auction. Judy was excited to see her ancestors' house and land, and we wanted to retrieve a couple of antique pieces before everything was gone for good.

On our way home we stopped at a piece-goods store where Judy chose a pattern and material, two months in advance of Hallowe'en, to make a costume for Forrest — so typical of her good planning and thoughtfulness. Arriving back home that evening, I reflected what a wonderful day we had had.

After supper Judy made several phone calls in connection with a Sunday School cookout, then sat down on the den floor, spread out the costume material, and cut out Forrest's Hallowe'en outfit. Around 9 o'clock she spoke with Rusty on the phone, expecting him to drive in from Alabama the next day in time for the cookout. Just before 11 o'clock another friend called about the cookout, and they laughed and talked together. After Judy hung up the phone, she came to my room to tell me who all was coming and what each couple was bringing to eat.

And Judy had made one last phone call that night. Even in her last hours, she still believed in her marriage and was preparing and planning for that trip with Rusty to Jacksonville. Concerned as to whether Rusty would be welcome in her sister's home, Judy called Becky to ask whether she and Stephen might have changed their minds, now that they had had time to think it over. Was Rusty still invited? Becky assured her that she and Stephen loved and supported her and would be available to her in whatever way she needed them to be. So, plans would continue as made. That night Judy seemed thoroughly happy.

We were all tired after our long day, however. Little Hunter was asleep. Judy and Forrest brushed their teeth in the bathroom next to my bedroom. I was already in bed, and Forrest kept running into my room, teasing his mom by saying he was "stealing kisses from MeMe."

Judy laughed and said over and over to him, "Don't give all my lovin's away." And then he would run to my bed and kiss me again and again. They left my room chasing each other down the stairs, laughing and giggling. Several times I heard her repeat to Forrest, "Don't give all my lovin's away." That was the last time I saw Judy alive.

At 2:00 A.M. I heard her come upstairs to get Hunter's bottle and warm it, then go back down. I keep remembering her last words: "Don't give all my lovin's away." Judy had so much love in her heart, it will never ever all be given away. It was around 3:30 A.M. that Forrest woke us and said, "MeMe, my mommy's dead."

A FAMILY IN SHOCK

❧ Immediately after my 911 call, we phoned Sanda in Gray, just seven miles away; Andy in Chattanooga; and Becky in Jacksonville, Florida. All Becky could say was, "No, Momma, no!" At our house the first police car arrived in minutes, followed by many law-enforcement people, rescue-squad personnel, and, in response to Kelver's call, his physician brother, Dr. Darrell Mullins. The scene was immediately taped off with yellow tape:

POLICE LINE - DO NOT CROSS

The first questions asked were, "What happened?" "Why was she outside?" "Did she have any enemies?" This last question was so absurd that, in the midst of my horror, I could not respond.

The police found no sign of burglary or theft, forced entry, or a struggle. Nothing was missing. Police dogs completely searched the surrounding area, finding a ring of keys to our Oldsmobile, and a single key under Judy's body, later identified as the key to her Nissan. Officers spent several more hours fingerprinting, taking photographs, videotaping, and lifting blood samples from the body, basement door, vehicles, and entire outside area.

Wondering how I had the strength to do it, I carried both boys upstairs and put them to bed. Forrest and Hunter immediately went back to sleep. Surely God was watching over and protecting them in a peaceful rest, at a time when everyone else was in such agonies of grief and shock. We had many difficult tasks ahead of us. In a matter of a very few hours, my vocabulary expanded tremendously. Legal terms and words I had never heard forced themselves into my consciousness.

Judy's Husband Is Told

Ͽ   After I telephoned Rusty's parents at 5:30 A.M., his dad offered to get in touch with Rusty in Birmingham. Judy had always been close to Rusty's parents, confiding in them her concerns about her marriage, since it was evident that Rusty was living miles away and leading a lifestyle that was not pleasing to any of us. Rusty's dad called back after about fifteen minutes, saying he had spoken with Rusty's roommate, that Rusty was not at home but was "out with friends."

About 7:00 A.M. Rusty finally called. He did not ask how we were, nor did he inquire about the children. Since we were emotionally shattered and physically unable to speak about the tragic events, we turned over the phone to one of the police detectives, who gave Rusty the details. Rusty's father, meanwhile, made arrangements for him to catch a plane to Tri-Cities from Birmingham.

Just minutes after finding our daughter, I had gone to the kitchen to see about Hunter's bottles. Opening the refrigerator, I found eight bottles that Judy had prepared, standing in a row. She had made the bottles before going to bed, getting a jump on the busy day ahead. I said out loud, "Thank you, God!"

Standing there in the kitchen, still scarcely able to function, I spied Judy's wedding band, engagement ring, and watch on the windowsill above the sink. She had never, ever removed her jewelry or left it so. I carried everything immediately to a safe place, thinking I would keep these things for her sons in the years ahead.

Urgent Matters To Be Faced

Ͽ   After that things moved very quickly. In Jacksonville a distraught Becky hurriedly made plans to come. Andrew in Chattanooga was living through his own nightmare. Months later, he was able to record his own moving version of that day:

> *In the blackness of that early Wednesday morning, I can remember my wife Tonya answering the phone and saying very little prior to hanging it back up. My first thought was an early-morning wrong number. Several times I asked who it was. Finally she said, "That was your mom. She says Judy has just committed suicide."*

Even though I heard, I didn't comprehend her words. After she told me what Mom had said, or at least what Tonya thought she had said, we both sat oblivious to reality as the words slowly sank in.

I remember calling my parents back. Mom immediately answered. I held the phone shakily to my ear, asking, "Did you just call? What's wrong?"

In agony, Mom said she had called, and she repeated the message, that she had found my sister Judy in the driveway, dead, lying in a pool of blood. Again, Mom said she believed it was a suicide. I stated emphatically that it could not have been. "I'm on my way," I said.

I laid the phone back in its cradle and sat staring into the deep darkness of our bedroom, in complete shock, hoping I would soon be awakening from a nightmare. Little did I realize how terribly nightmares can come true. The next little while became a blur, for our lives were about to change forever.

I repeated to Tonya what Mom had said. Mom had told me the police and ambulance had been summoned. Again, my wife and I sat for several minutes in total disbelief. I have never felt so confused in all my life. All of a sudden it seemed that I had lost control of myself, my surroundings, my life.

In the years that I had been a police officer, I had been involved in nearly every type of crime imaginable, including suicides and murders. I had just heard words spoken that I had heard many times before, but never had I heard them concerning my own flesh and blood. For that, I would learn, one can never be prepared.

Even though I was brought up to honor God and in all things good and bad to trust Him, I can honestly say that God was not even a thought this early in the morning. Perhaps a thousand times, as I put on my clothes and made preparations to leave, the words heard over the phone echoed in my mind — still they seemed like a bad dream.

I hurried to the kitchen and picked up the phone, realizing that this trip to Johnson City from Chattanooga — a distance of some 200 miles — would be like no other. I was already wishing I were there at the scene and at my parents' side. I was remembering the few times as an officer when a dispatcher would radio me that a citizen had an emergency or sick child and needed an escort to a doctor or hospital. In such cases we would assist in any way that we could.

And so that morning I called the Tennessee Highway Patrol. My call just "happened" to be answered by a friend I had long known from police academy days. I told him not to say anything, just to listen to every word. I told him I was leaving for Johnson City going to a murder scene, what vehicle I would be driving, and that I did not intend to stop. Before he could respond, I hung up.

As I ran out the door, I wondered to myself, Why did you say a murder scene? My instincts and years of training were beginning to take charge, and my actions were automatic.

As I entered the ramp to I-75 north, my emergency lights flashing, there were no vehicles in sight and absolutely no movement around me. It was still not yet 6:30 A.M. For the first time that morning, thoughts of God entered my conscious process, and they were selfish thoughts — God, get me to Johnson City, and hurry! It wasn't a request, but a command.

As my truck seemed to be on automatic pilot, precious scenes began flooding my mind — childhood memories, Christmases past, birthday parties, the home we had lived in, and hundreds of other such scenes. As I topped the hill going into Cleveland, the sudden appearance of blue lights ahead brought me back to reality. Great, a speeding ticket, I thought, noting that my speedometer was above 100 miles per hour. I said to myself: Officer, you'll have to follow me, because I'm not stopping.

As I quickly closed the gap between us, the police car pulled out in front of me amid a cloud of dirt and dust. I could see the officer waving to me and looking at me through his mirror, clearly meaning, "Let's go. I'm your escort."

For the first time, I broke into tears and finally said, "Thank you, Lord." The highway patrolman led me with full lights and siren for nearly 40 miles. We were traveling between 100 and 110 miles per hour. At the Sweetwater exit, he pulled over, giving me a thumbs-up as I passed. I was profoundly grateful for his efforts and for the friend who had made it possible for me to proceed on.

A mile later, as I crested another hill, blue lights again appeared on the horizon. Again a police officer, this time in a Loudon County Sheriff's Department car, took over the escort. We continued to the Knox County line and picked up a county officer. A few miles later, another Tennessee Highway Patrol car took the lead, as the three of us sped around the Knoxville bypass dodging early-morning rush-hour traffic. Even though I wondered what people thought with all the action, I didn't care. Knoxvillians were on their way to work and attending to their daily rituals. For once, I would miss going to work myself.

The emergency escorts continued all the way to the Washington County line, with two other departments taking part. Each time the officers pulled off, they saluted, all waving as they left me to continue carrying out their individual duties.

As I entered Washington County outside of Greeneville, I wondered where my escort was, now selfishly expecting a private parade. I learned later that every county police car was at the house where I had grown up since the fifth grade, parked in disarray, each officer busy about urgent tasks and assisting in every way they could to solve this terrible crisis that my own family was going through.

As I pulled into my parents' driveway, I realized that my life had now changed forever but little knew what shocking events would unfold in the next few months and years. I had driven 204 miles in exactly two hours, averaging over 100 miles per hour. Most of the trip, I don't remember. Bits and pieces I shall never forget.

I later thanked the Lord for His leadership and guidance, with a special thank-you for those highway patrolmen and police officers who assisted me without my even asking for their help. In every person's life, there is always one day that can never be forgotten. Mine is September 7, 1994.

Other travelers besides Andy were on the road that morning as well. Rusty's parents came as fast as they could. They, too, were in shock, and we wept together, trying to imagine how anyone could want to harm our precious Judy. Of course I had realized that Judy would not have killed herself, with those two precious babies in her devoted care.

Rusty's mother helped me fold up the pattern pieces and material for Forrest's Hallowe'en outfit that Judy had left spread out in the den, offering to take it all home to finish for our grandson. Rusty's parents stayed with us all day, leaving just long enough to go to the airport to meet Rusty's flight and drive him to the police department to be interviewed. When they returned with him to our house, he was carrying just an overnight bag, and I noticed he was not wearing his wedding band.

That night he called his roommate in Alabama and asked him to send his suit by bus, adding, "Oh, by the way, go in my bedroom, look in my jewelry box, and get my wedding band. I guess I'd better wear it." Why wasn't he wearing it to begin with?

Friends and relatives started to arrive, taking charge of the kitchen and baby-sitting. Someone answered the phone, noting every call. What strength these friends provided!

Judy's body was taken away for an autopsy, then released to the funeral home. Making arrangements by phone, we were advised by a good friend who was also a funeral-home employee that we should bring an outfit for Judy that had a high collar and long sleeves. At that, we quickly resolved that her casket would remain closed.

Adjusting To What Was

⁓ Ever since she had been with us, Judy had kept one change of children's clothes and fresh diapers upstairs for convenience. When Sanda arrived, she offered to dress the boys and went to look for these clothes, then came back in a flash asking me to come. Pointing to the antique baby bed where we kept the extra clothes, she showed me six carefully selected outfits for each child. Judy had seen to it that her sons' needs would be met for all the days of their upcoming trip.

That Wednesday was the busiest day of my life. I was faced with the need to notify people, comfort family members and receive their consolation in return, check the refrigerator for the children's food, inventory the diapers, work out things with the funeral home, and take phone calls from everywhere.

A Child's Recall

🍃   We soon saw that the authorities would have to talk with Forrest. Fortunately, this bright little boy was calm and willing to tell his Uncle Andy exactly what he had seen, as the detectives looked on. He said two men had been there, one of them a person he remembered who had played basketball with his dad. On hearing that, we had to wonder what Rusty knew. Forrest also told Andy one of the two men was dark and wore a red hat and tennis shoes.

During the previous night a heavy dew had settled on the freshly cut grass, and Forrest told his Uncle Andy, "I told the man he better not bring that grass in here on my MeMe's carpet. My momma tried to kick that man," he declared, giving Andy a pretend kick in the leg to demonstrate. Andy could hardly bear to hear the little fellow tell what he had seen.

Later Forrest asked me why everyone was crying. I explained that everyone was sad because his momma was gone, and that our family members and friends were coming to be with us to help us when we felt so sad.

A Family And A Community Reach Out

🍃   My brothers were called. In shock and disbelief, Webster, a missionary in Uganda, said, "I'm on the next plane." Dan, a retired missionary living in Texas, and Arthur, in West Virginia, told us they were on the way. My missionary nephew in Singapore, Charles Carroll, called and prayed with us on the phone.

My husband's brothers and sisters were also called and told us they would soon be with us. Of Judy's thirty-one cousins, twenty-one came, and those who were unable to come called and sent messages of love and support. Every one has been to visit us since then.

Our family's tragic loss touched thousands of people, many we did not even know. As word of the horror spread, everyone felt as great a sense of shock as our own family. Such things just did not happen in our town, and they just did not happen to families like ours. For days, a steady stream of family and friends came and went. Hundreds arrived bringing food, flowers, and memorials to "little Judy," as she was called by so many.

Our kitchen was stocked with enough fresh fruits, vegetables, meats, breads, and desserts to feed an army. Our pantry was running over with paper goods, canned items, and soft drinks. For weeks afterward, I had no need to go to the grocery store. The generosity of so many simply overwhelmed us.

Early one morning I answered the doorbell to be met by two employees of the nearby supermarket carrying huge bags, filled to the brim. I invited them in and saw that they had brought breakfast foods and paper goods in abundance. One of these ladies asked if she could lead a prayer. Of course I agreed. Sanda came in and held hands in a circle with the three of us as our visitor prayed. We were deeply touched by the genuineness of her prayer as she asked God to be with us all. Afterward she asked for a pencil and paper to write down other things we could use — baby formula, baby food, diapers. An hour later two men came from the same store bearing two large boxes of items covering the baby's every conceivable need.

JUDY'S LAST GIFTS

ઠ▲ On the day after Judy's death, as Sanda and Becky were dressing the boys, one of Forrest's shoes rolled under the guest-room bed. Becky lifted the dust ruffle and made another stunning find — Christmas presents Judy had bought for each member of the Mullins and Freels families. Every niece, nephew, uncle, aunt, sister, brother, and parent was remembered; each yet-to-be-wrapped gift had a stick-on tag with the intended recipient's name. We all had a good cry and then lowered the dust ruffle again, leaving the precious packages for the time being. Later, Sanda took charge of these special treasures, carefully wrapping and marking them, "From Forrest and Hunter."

FUNERAL PLANS TO BE MADE

ઠ▲ All our strength was required to deal with Judy's funeral arrangements. Our dear friend at the funeral home made it all as smooth as possible for us, although he, too, was deeply affected by our tragedy. Even so, when the time came to select a casket, I wasn't sure I could go through with that most difficult task.

To my astonishment, just before we were to enter the casket room,

Rusty suddenly fell to the floor, sobbing as if his heart would break. None of us knew quite what to do. Kelver, Sanda, Becky, and I went on ahead without him, and when we came to a beautiful lavender-gray casket with white porcelain handles trimmed with violets, we agreed that this was the right choice. I went back for Rusty, who nodded in seeming approval, then returned with us to the conference room where he was given a statement of costs to sign. He was hesitant, but eventually he wrote his name at the bottom.

The next trial was choosing a burial plot. As we looked at various spots in the cemetery, Rusty seemed unable to make a decision. Becky favored a beautiful knoll directly across from a church school, and when we heard the children's laughter from the playground, she declared, "This is it. This is Judy's spot." We were all grateful for Becky's strength at that difficult time. Afterward, in the office, Rusty signed for two spaces — one for Judy, the second presumably for himself.

THE ASSURANCE OF GOD'S WORD

֍ In the great emotional pain of these terrible decisions, we longed for comfort and felt led to read particular Bible verses. Romans 8:37-39 gave us the greatest measure of hope:

> *No, in all these things we are more than conquerors through him who loved us. For I am convinced that neither death, nor life, nor angels, nor rulers, nor things present, nor things to come, nor powers, nor height, nor depth, nor anything else in all creation will be able to separate us from the love of God in Christ Jesus our Lord.*

OUR LAST FAREWELL

֍ On Friday the funeral-home people called to say all arrangements were complete and asked whether we wanted to view Judy's body. Rusty and his parents, Andy and Tonya, and Becky and Stephen wanted to go, while Sanda and Shannon chose to stay at home with Forrest and Hunter and the other children. Although Kelver and I didn't expect to view the body, we decided at least to accompany our children to the funeral home.

When we arrived, Andy was so upset that I suggested it might be better for him not to see Judy. He refused, saying he didn't want his last memory of his little sister to be the awful one of her lying in the driveway. I was so proud of him for his fortitude.

Kelver and I waited in the foyer as the others went in. Then Andy, after seeing the body, came back with outstretched arms, motioning us to come in as well, which we did. I am very grateful for that moment. Afterward we asked the attendants to seal the casket.

Rusty sat down on a huge wingback chair and began sobbing again.

Becky knelt down on the floor beside him to ask straightforwardly, "What are you thinking, Rusty?"

"If I had only been home to protect my wife, this never would have happened."

Becky spoke firmly to her brother-in-law. "Rusty, you know that Judy loved you till death did you part." I suspected this was Becky's way of reminding Rusty what a faithful, loving wife her sister Judy had been, that she knew Judy had never stopped believing in him and their marriage, while his commitment was anything but sure.

"I know," was all the answer Rusty gave.

No Answers Yet

In the days afterward, we had to deal with the aftermath of a brutal, heinous crime in addition to the other expected matters that follow upon any death. We had already had to deal with the harsh reality of the earliest headlines:

Johnson City Woman Found Stabbed to Death
Authorities Seeking Motive in Stabbing Death
Local Murder Victim Led Quiet Christian Life

Leaving the murder investigation to the authorities, we soon learned that power-company employees had found knives and bloody gloves in a ditch about a mile from our home, but nothing more had been discovered. The newspapers picked this up:

Murder Weapons Recovered

Many in the community feared that a crazed random killer was at large, and feelings were running high.

Our most immediate task, however, was arranging for Judy's funeral and burial services. Judy's pastor had just relocated and could not take part, and as our family talked together, we immediately thought of our brother-in-law, Dr. Joe Stacker of the Baptist Sunday School Board in Nashville. As we were discussing calling Joe, the telephone rang. I answered, and it was Joe himself. I explained that we were getting ready to call him to see whether he could conduct the funeral.

"That's why I'm calling," he said, "to offer any help that I can."

A CELEBRATION OF LIFE

When the time came for the funeral, we took little Forrest and Hunter to the church nursery where they remained with other family children. It was the ideal place for them, watched over by loving caregivers whom they knew well. Four weeks earlier, Judy had helped us plan her grandmother's memorial service. Now we followed a similar service for Judy, calling it "A Celebration Of Life."

When we entered the church that evening, every seat was taken, and many stood in the foyer and aisles. Hundreds joined us in singing beloved favorites: "Blessed Assurance," "Like A River Glorious," and "How Great Thou Art." The Rev. William Carter, interim pastor of the church, read Judy's favorite Bible passage — I Corinthians, Chapter 13 — and prayed. We felt our Lord very near us at that time.

Joe Stacker's funeral sermon was honest and comforting. He began:

> *I don't know about you, but I don't want to be here tonight. I have asked myself over and over, why? Why did Judy have to die? Why did she die so brutally? Don't tell me God needed this mother of two boys in Heaven. I have no answer to this perplexing question, except the presence and power of evil. As long as evil invades people's minds and hearts, events such as Judy's murder will occur . . . .*

Drawing on the beloved Twenty-Third Psalm, he went on to offer us the comfort of our Christian faith, that God is always with us, God provides for us even in the worst of circumstances, the light of hope is always there among life's darkness, and we have God's promise to take us to be with Him at the last.

The service ended beautifully and simply as we listened to Judy's recorded voice singing her Seed Company solo, "To Know the Heart of Jesus," trusting that she was singing her highest praise that evening around the Throne.

SUSPICIONS ARISE

ਵ੍ਹ The following morning as we approached the cemetery for the burial, the church bell across the way tolled the hour of ten — another very emotional moment. After Judy's body had been laid to rest, a group from an area church served lunch to all family and friends who wished to attend. It was a time of remembering, wondering, shedding tears, and being grateful that loved ones could come together at such a difficult moment.

As a part of their continuing investigation, the police had received our permission to have plainclothes officers at the funeral and burial. Among the hundreds of mourners who came were Rusty's two room-mates from Birmingham, one of them with a large, very noticeable scratch on one side of his jaw. Both attended the funeral, the burial, and the lunch afterward. The young man with the scratch, Claude Kenny, had come to our house back in the summer to pick up a bed at Rusty's request. On this occasion, at least three members of our family remarked how guilty he looked and wondered whether he had been involved.

FAMILY LIFE GOES ON

ਵ੍ਹ In the afternoon, Andy made the welcome suggestion that he and Tonya, Rusty, Becky and Stephen, and Sanda and Shannon take all the grandchildren to the park to run, play, and unwind — a welcome release from the tension and sadness. It was our granddaughter Amber's ninth birthday, with our grandson Drew's sixth to follow in two days. Although Andy and Tonya had explained to their children that we could not celebrate birthdays at this time, they had been promised parties after they returned home. Young as they were, the children understood.

After they went out, Kelver and I found ourselves alone for the first time in days. The house was extremely quiet — no police, no family, no guests. Remembering that Judy had already wrapped birthday gifts for her niece and nephew, I suddenly exclaimed to Kelver, "Let's have a birthday party!" He was startled but quickly agreed it was the right thing to do.

I went to my supply closet and got out a birthday tablecloth. Together we set the table for all our family and ordered pizza for supper. I arranged gifts for both children, and all was in readiness when our flock returned from the park. How surprised they were when we burst out singing "Happy Birthday!" at the top of our lungs.

As the children opened their packages and read Judy's cards, everyone cried, including Rusty. Kelver said a prayer asking God to bless Drew and Amber. Even under the cloud of our sorrow, this was simultaneously a joyous family time. We knew Judy would have wanted us to do just as we did, and I believe firmly that it was the first step to a deeper healing for us all.

On Sunday morning Rusty wanted to go to church, so he, Andy, Kelver and I went together. It was strange sitting in the same place I had sat just two days earlier for the funeral. Judy and I had always shared a hymnbook — she sang alto and I sang soprano — our voices blending as one. Now I realized Judy would never hold the book to sing with me again. After the service Judy's friends crowded around, hugging us, crying, sharing their sorrow with ours. Everyone showed great concern for Rusty in the loss of his young wife.

On Monday Rusty asked me to go with him to visit Judy's grave. We took little Hunter along, and while Rusty knelt quietly by the grave for about ten minutes, I carried Hunter a little distance away to allow my son-in-law his private moment. When Rusty stood up and started back toward the car I followed, wondering what was going through his mind.

Looking For Clues

❧ Now additional daily bulletins poured in:

Four Detectives Working 16 Hours A Day on the Judy Mullins Freels Murder Case Reward Offered in Brutal Stabbing Death

We met repeatedly with news media and criminal investigators, hoping the reward would bring results. Questions, phone calls, pictures, fingerprinting, and affidavits overshadowed our shock at the horrid reality of Judy's death, our grief that her precious little son had seen it all. I noticed that whenever reporters were present, Rusty appeared devastated, but as soon as they packed up their gear and left, he became his usually composed self again. It had been the same at the funeral home — extreme appearances of grief whenever others were present, composure afterward. I found this very odd.

Area law-enforcement agencies formed a special multi-agency homicide task force to intensify the search for Judy's killer — Johnson City's Police Department, Washington County's Sheriff's Department, the Tennessee Bureau of Investigation, and the 1st Judicial District Attorney General's Office. Johnson City's Chief of Police made a statement to the press: "We've pulled out all the stops . . . . this is a priority case for us." People still could not believe such a thing had happened in our nice quiet town. The newspapers were full of it, and all television channels carried updated reports several times each day.

A CLIMATE OF UNEASE

❧   As our children left to return to their homes, all voiced concern for our safety. Rusty stayed on, sleeping in the upstairs guest bedroom with his sons. None of us went downstairs for days. My first thought was to protect my family — Judy's sons and dad and, yes, myself. Having no idea who had committed this murder, we all feared that something terrible might happen to someone else in the household. On the chance that the killers might come back looking for Forrest, who had told the police what he knew, he was never left alone for a moment. Unmarked police cars patrolled our street, and various authorities called frequently to let us know we were being protected.

With our phone ringing from early morning until late at night, Rusty became quite irritable: "Can't people just leave us alone?" I told him these were precious friends and family, expressing their very real love, support, and concern. Five days after Judy was buried, he decided to leave the children with us and go to Alabama to get his car and some more clothes. Kelver was to drive him part of the way, then Rusty's dad would take over, then Andy, so that no one had to drive the entire distance to Birmingham. Moments after Kelver and Rusty left, the detectives called wanting to speak to him.

A Break In The Case

& A little over a week after Judy's murder, the police brought us some truly shocking news. Two Birmingham men had been arrested after a young woman told authorities she believed her 25-year-old brother, Claude Oliver Kenny III, had been involved in the murder. He was the same young man we had seen at the funeral with the scratch on his face, the one who had come to our house earlier in the year. When TBI officers went to Birmingham to question him and asked to search his car, he consented and signed a search waiver, after which they found a shopping bag and sales slip from a Johnson City discount store for two pairs of gloves purchased just hours before the killing. Further searches made with Kenny's consent yielded boots and a towel with what looked like bloodstains, and a sales slip from an area store for two knives.

Ongoing conversations led to Kenny's voluntary confession implicating two other men, a former co-worker named Raytheon Harris, also 25, and a 29-year-old man named — Russell Fredrick Freels. After his arrest in Birmingham on September 16, Kenny stated that he and Harris had stopped at a store outside Johnson City and bought two knives before buying the gloves in town. He also told how the murder occurred and that he and Harris had returned to Birmingham immediately afterward. After being implicated by Kenny, Harris was arrested on the same day in Alabama and, being advised of his rights, also willingly confessed to participation in the murder. The two waived extradition and were transported back to East Tennessee.

A Promised Reward

& According to Kenny, Russell had instigated a murder-for-hire plot in order to collect on his wife's life insurance, amounting to $240,000. Kenny stated that he had been promised $50,000 in exchange for the crime, that on his own he had enlisted Harris to help him in exchange for half of his own reward, and that he had been told to kill three people — Judy, Kelver, and me — but not to harm the little boys. Our blood ran cold as we realized what danger we had been in.

The police told us that Rusty had been a prime suspect from the start, and they had done extremely careful investigative work until they were sure they had all they needed for his arrest. On September 19, twelve days after his wife's murder, Rusty was again interviewed by Johnson City police and subsequently arrested, even though he continued to deny any involvement in the crime. All three suspects, charged with first-degree murder in Judy's death and conspiracy to kill my husband and me, were held without bond in the Washington County Jail. Kenny and Harris were also charged with especially aggravated burglary for unlawfully entering our home with the intent of killing my husband and me.

Although Kenny and Harris confessed, saying that Rusty had agreed to provide an alibi, Rusty categorically denied any part in it, even when confronted with statements the other two had made to the police and tape-recorded conversations between Kenny and himself about his involvement. Later statements contributed by various women and men who had had dealings with the three corroborated Kenny's contention that Rusty had long talked about having Judy killed and was the instigator of the plot.

Immediately the police issued a press release, and the headlines told the news:

Husband, Pair Charged With Murder
Murder For Hire Alleged in Johnson City Slaying

After that our community breathed easier, assured there were no random murderers on the loose — only three accused killers with a known motive, locked up tight in the county jail. In the wake of the three arrests, District Attorney General David Crockett told reporters that the crime was "the most brutal, unnecessary, and uncalled-for crime" he had ever prosecuted. "Nothing in my recollection is more stunning and more devastating," he said. And privately he told our family he would do everything he could to make the ordeal ahead as easy as possible for us.

CHILLING CONFESSIONS

ₐ   The details of Kenny's and Harris's confessions were horrifying. Kenny stated he and Harris had driven by our house several times in the afternoon and evening of September 6, once while Kelver was mowing the lawn, and again after dark when our lights were still on, waiting until everybody was asleep.

Kenny said because Judy knew him, he felt confident she would come out of the house if he woke her by knocking at her open bedroom window, telling her his car had broken down and he needed a tire iron.

By his account, Judy did get up and come out, offering him the tire iron from her car. Kenny said he told her the tire iron wouldn't fit his car, so Judy went back for my car keys in order to obtain a tire iron from it. And when she couldn't find one in my car, she offered Kenny the use of her own car.

This story had to be true, for anyone who knew Judy knew that she would do anything she could to help someone, even in the middle of the night.

Even more chilling was Kenny's statement that Rusty had given him a complete diagram of our house with instructions where to find our valuables. Kenny said that he and Harris had intended to burglarize our home after murdering us all, to make it appear we had been killed in a robbery. All his information was accurate — information he could only have obtained from Rusty, who knew where our valuables were kept. And this young man had actually been inside our house with our knowledge, just weeks before.

Harris's confession substantiated Kenny's, for he stated that when Judy returned with the second set of keys and opened the trunk of my car, Kenny grabbed and held her from behind while Harris stabbed her in the side and abdomen so that her intestines spilled out, after which she collapsed. In the midst of this violence, Harris stated, Forrest awoke and came outside, and Harris picked the child up and carried him back to bed, because Rusty had said not to harm the boys. Harris stated he had then gone partway up the stairs intending to kill Kelver and me until he realized that Kenny wasn't with him, at which point he turned and went back outside to find Judy dying or dead, her throat slashed, and Kenny waiting for him at his car.

Police interrogations of the pair also revealed that on two earlier occasions, Kenny had traveled to Tennessee for the purpose of carrying out these killings, once on July 10 when he made it to Johnson City on a motorcycle, and again on July 17 in company with another man, although the car they were driving broke down so that they couldn't carry out their plan — blood-curdling revelations.

Illustrations

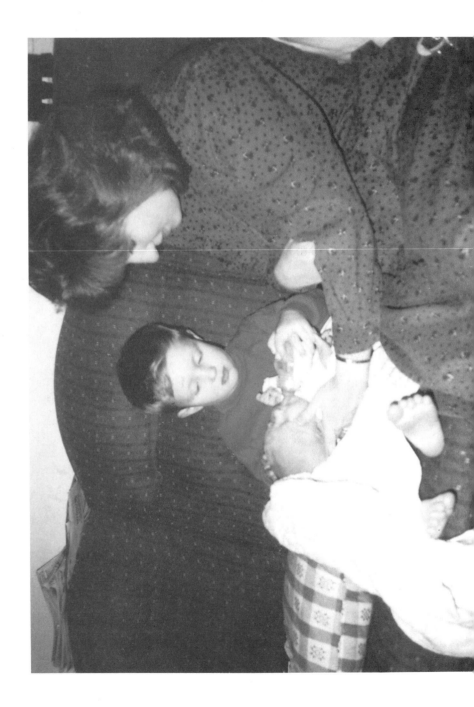

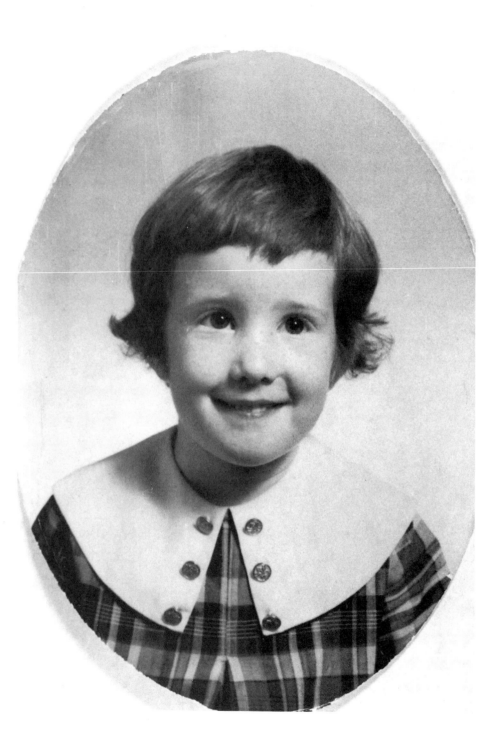

Part Two

ACCEPTING THE FUTURE

❧   With Rusty in jail, Kelver and I accepted responsibility for the funeral and burial expenses. We reserved an additional space at the cemetery next to Judy so that, instead of Rusty, the two of us could eventually be buried beside her. We ordered a marker for the grave with Judy's name, dates of birth and death, and the title of her special song, "To Know the Heart of Jesus."

Two months afterward came Thanksgiving — a trying time for us all. At our family dinner we felt an emptiness, with Judy gone and Rusty behind bars. Together, we prayed, asking God for continued strength to lead us into an uncertain future.

When Christmas arrived, we thankfully accepted Andy's and Tonya's invitation to spend the holiday with them in Chattanooga. All seventeen of us came together there, eating, laughing, crying, praying, singing, sharing memories of past years and speculations about the days ahead. The children especially had many questions, some of which were very difficult to answer. Forrest and Hunter also spent part of the holidays with their Freels grandparents.

THE WHEELS OF JUSTICE

❧   For many weeks and months of that terrible autumn, winter, and early spring, seemingly endless legal proceedings went on. We made trip after trip to courtrooms for various hearings. In February, both Kenny and Harris pleaded guilty to first-degree murder and conspiracy to commit first-degree murder, in exchange for sentences of life in prison plus 25 years, rather than the death sentences they might have received had they not cooperated with the authorities or entered guilty pleas. Their sentences remained undisclosed, however, pending the outcome of Rusty's separate trial. According to a later news report in the *Johnson City Press*, attorneys speculated that they might be eligible for parole in approximately 37 years.

Finally, in April, Rusty requested a plea-bargain hearing and also entered his own guilty plea, choosing life in prison without parole rather than undergoing a death-penalty prosecution. The headlines this time were conclusive:

Although Kelver and I had always wanted Rusty to have every benefit of the law, we were thankful to be spared the ordeal of such a trial with the attendant publicity, reopening of wounds that were still terribly painful, and the long-drawn-out appeals likely to follow. Knowing the lengthy sentences that Rusty and the other two would serve provided some measure of closure for our ordeal.

ACCEPTING THE TRUTH

After this plea-bargain hearing Rusty asked to speak with Kelver and me. We agreed to see him and were ushered into a small conference room, along with Rusty's father, the county sheriff, and a bailiff. Rusty told us about the alcohol, drugs, and affairs that had destroyed his marriage and how he had drifted away from his wife. He acknowledged that he had asked Kenny to "arrange an accident," but said he didn't think he would do it until he saw the scratch on Kenny's face at the funeral. Then, Rusty said, "I knew he had done it. I couldn't turn him in, because I knew he would tell on me." We could scarcely believe we were hearing our son-in-law speak to us about arranging our daughter's death.

A FATHER'S CHRISTIAN FORGIVENESS

With great dignity, Kelver responded. "I have forgiven you, Rusty," he said. "I have worked through this, and for my own sake I have forgiven you. I have loved you as a son-in-law and have enjoyed having you to be a part of our family. I'm going to miss you and I'm sorry you will not be here to play golf with me." He went on to thank Rusty for making the decision about a plea bargain without going through with a trial.

Rusty told us the reality of his deeds didn't really hit him until he underwent psychological testing in jail and was told the results. He cried again, saying, "I have a lot of problems, and I am not sure what I can do about them."

As we prepared to leave, he told us that if other family members wanted to adopt the two boys and give them a new last name, he would sign papers giving permission. "This is no reflection on our family name," he told his dad. "But if it's best, I would agree."

In parting, Kelver said, "Rusty, we will never see Judy again on this earth, and I just want you to know that we will never see you again." He shook Rusty's hand, and as we stood to leave I hugged him, unable to hold back the tears, grieving for a son-in-law and the father of our two precious grandchildren.

HEALING FOR JUDY'S SONS

As Rusty suggested, one of our other children gladly adopted the boys, providing them with a loving, attentive, Christian home. Forrest underwent a long course of counseling at a mental-health center and has come out well. Hunter is growing and is just the sort of boy he should be. They have various opportunities to remember Judy, visiting the cemetery, making her favorite cake on her birthday, talking about her in a very natural way. Forrest talks about her a great deal and sometimes refers to her as "My momma up in Heaven." His counselors told us to keep her pictures out, let them watch home videos, and never shrink from mentioning her.

I had already given Forrest one framed picture of Judy, and after I gave him another — her bridal picture in a silver frame — he carried the first picture into Hunter's room and set it up there, placing the new one on his own dresser. After that, Hunter would go to his room and look at his picture and say, "Mommy." One night he motioned to hold it, and when it was given to him, he smiled, kissed the picture, and said, "Night, night, Mommy."

These moments are not easy for the adults who love and care for these precious boys, but we know that God can comfort us and give us strength.

MEMORIALS THAT ENDURE

Many memorials have been given in Judy's name, including a large complete outdoor playground at one church and an avenue of pink and white dogwoods leading to another church. Our son Andy came up with a wonderful idea that many are continuing to participate in — a memorial scholarship at Carson-Newman College. He had been waking up in the middle of the night praying about how to go about setting it up, genuinely excited by the possibilities. With good counsel from the college development office, this scholarship has become a reality — the Judy Mullins Freels Memorial Scholarship. The fund continues to grow, with proceeds from the sale of this book adding to it. A page in back of this book gives details about the scholarship fund.

Many deserving young people will be the beneficiaries, a permanent reminder of Judy's achievements and a continuation in other lives of her own witness of faith. At the ceremony officially announcing the scholarship, Kelver declared, "I pray that this school, through the years, will help to carry on something that Judy always wanted to do. That was to see people come to know Him in a closer way . . . . Her life's purpose was to know the heart of Jesus."

SHARING OUR HEALING WITH THE WORLD

❧ In the years since Judy's death, Kelver and I have had many opportunities to speak to scores of community and civic groups and churches. We are always amazed to hear how many other people have great troubles and deep hurts, and it really helps us to be able to share our experiences with them. We continue to be in awe of how God uses instances in our lives to touch someone else. We have been blessed in the opportunity to try to console and comfort many of Judy's friends who have found it terribly difficult to move beyond this tragedy into healing.

With God's help, our family has walked through the valley without dwelling there permanently. I had never, ever thought of burying one of my children, and it had never occurred to me that my youngest child would die before I did. She had so many things planned. She was far too young to die.

MY OWN JOURNEY TOWARD HEALING

❧ Strangely enough, part of my recovery has come through the process of sorting through all of Judy's belongings and mementos. Tears flowed again as I did this with other family members, and it helped me to heal. Another part of my healing, a great part, has come about through the process of writing this book. As the words have flowed out, healing grace has flowed in.

SCRIPTURE AND COMPASSION PROVIDE STRENGTH

❧ Knowing that healing can only come about through complete forgiveness, Kelver and I and the rest of our family members have searched
the Scriptures and prayed daily for the Lord's help. For me, forgiveness
began with acceptance — accepting the reality that Judy died, accepting
the truth that her husband caused her death, accepting the fact that
neither one is here in our midst any longer. Forgiveness is difficult.
Forgiveness is also possible. It is something we have to learn, something
we have to discover, something we have to receive.

When the loss is so great, when the pain so hard, when the bitterness runs so deep, how can one forgive? How can one cope when a
family, friends, and a community are all so devastated? For me, the
secret has been to rely on God to help me work through it. Special
Scripture passages have been a great help. All these encouraging words
give strength:

Psalm 46:1 – *God is our refuge and strength.*

Psalm 8:2b – *Thou hast founded a bulwark because of thy foes, to
still the enemy and the avenger.*

Matthew 6:14-15 – *For if you forgive men their trespasses, your
heavenly Father also will forgive you; but if you do not forgive
men their trespasses, neither will your Father forgive your
trespasses.*

Matthew 18:21-22 – *Then Peter came up and said to him, "Lord,
how often shall my brother sin against me and I forgive him?
As many as seven times?" Jesus said to him, "I do not say to
you seven times, but seventy times seven."*

Philippians 2:12-13 – *Work out the salvation that God has given you
with a proper sense of awe and responsibility. For it is God who
is at work within you, giving you the will and power to achieve
this purpose.*

As I have struggled to come to grips with my feelings over these
months and years, I have felt every emotion that could be associated
with death: disbelief, shock, anger, shame, frustration, denial, bereave-
ment, bitterness. The list goes on and on, and sometimes I feel each
emotion all over again.

Throughout the forty years of Kelver's pastorates and my support, we had ministered to many in situations of crisis, deaths, and bereavements. Now it was different. Not only had the sting of death touched our lives, but the stigma of how it happened was devastating. We knew that we had to surrender to all the things in this life that were beyond our control, to ask for forgiveness and healing, to accept the comfort and consolation others offered to us.

One thing of which we can never be convinced is that it was God's will for our daughter to die at such a young age. We do not believe the loving God we serve makes such terrible demands on any of his children. Judy was killed by persons acting on motives we can never fully fathom. The only explanation we can accept is the one Joe Stacker offered at the funeral — that Judy's death was the result of the evil inevitably present in the world.

ACCEPTING THE PERSON WE NEVER REALLY KNEW

ᨏ Beyond that, after hearing the professionals' psychological report on my son-in-law, I learned that I needed to seek to understand Rusty. He was a very different person from the person we thought we knew, the man we and Judy thought she had married. I recognize that there is much I may never understand. This effort to understand does not mean that I excuse what he has done. It means only that I see, feel, and accept what is.

When I think of Rusty, which is every day, I remember the young man I thought I knew, the kind words, the courtship, the wedding vows, his prayers at our table, the father of his sons, the fun-loving son-in-law who would rather play golf than eat, a person with many friends who seemed a friend to all. Seeing him enter the courtroom in jail garb, shackles and bonds, I found it hard to believe this was the same good-looking bridegroom who had stood at the front of our church promising to love and cherish our daughter forever.

Now, as I think of him serving life without parole, my prayer is twofold: that he can begin to understand his addictive disease and take steps to overcome it, and that he has accepted or will one day genuinely accept Christ and come to know the Lord's own forgiveness and healing power in his life.

A Change Leading To Peace

🕊 Gradually Kelver and I saw that this house where we had lived for so long was too filled with painful reminders for us. We knew we had to leave old hurts behind. Thus, two years after Judy's death, and with much prayer and deliberation, we decided to move and soon found an ideal house just three miles away. Even though it was hard to leave a place our family had called home for thirty years, the rest of the family helped us with the tasks of relocation, and we have found a wonderful welcome in the new neighborhood. Truly God has provided for us and protected us in a marvelous way, and we know that He will continue to do so as we live.

God's Love Is Always Here

🕊 If you, too, have lived through a tragedy or a deep wound, my hope is that hearing my family's story may offer encouragement, lead you to a greater reliance on our Lord's eternal promises, and bring healing to your heart. For, after all, life is for the living, and no matter how dark the valleys may be that we have to walk through, I know that God does help us pass through the shadows and beyond, to a life of abundance and joy.

How I Explained To A Therapist
Some of the Issues I Had to Work Through

Q: Mattie, experts in psychology lately talk a lot about how we don't get punished *for* our anger but rather get punished *by* our anger: what it does to our bodies, what it does to tear us down. What did you find that your feelings did to you, emotionally and physically, before you were able to work your way through?

A: Well, at first we were all so shocked and stunned, and my first question was, Who could do this? Who in the world could do this to our Judith? And then your mind just goes rampant, you know, as to who. At the beginning we felt that it was just a random act, by somebody who just came through. We had no idea that it could be related to anybody we knew. All I thought at first was, Who could do this? So at first I wouldn't call it anger. It was grief — not knowing who it was.

Q: Are you saying it was hard to be angry when you couldn't focus on a person?

A: That's right. We were all so stunned that at that point I wouldn't have called it anger.

Q: How much time passed before you found out who it was?

A: After a few days we began to have a suspicion that Russell was involved with it someway, or that it was someone that he knew. It was one week later when the authorities went to Birmingham and got the confessions of the other two, and by the time they came back to Johnson City and arrested Russell, it was only about ten days.

Q: What were your feelings when you found out it was Russell?

A: It was just almost something you could not accept. And yet we had to. Of course, at that point I was mad, and I did have anger. There's no way of getting around it. But it was at that point when I had to really ask God to help me. Because I knew that I had to control that. I knew that I had to be an example to my family and to other people. I *wanted* to be. And that's when I prayed so hard that God would just help me.

Q: What was your prayer?

A: Just that somehow God would see me through it. That he would give me the strength to get through it, and to handle that anger. We all have anger, that's just a normal thing, but we all have to control it.

Q: I assume the anger didn't go away overnight.

A: Oh, no!

Q: How long did you have to struggle with this anger?

A: For weeks. The legal proceedings had started, and as we went into all of that, each day made it more real to us. And I still kept saying, How could he do this? Of course, knowing the alcohol and the drug situation and his going with other women, I had to realize that all of that was a factor.

Q: Did you think there were other factors in addition to the alcohol and other drugs?

A: I knew that there was a woman he was seeing. We had just learned she was pregnant and was going to have his baby, and we didn't know how in the world he was going to explain that or live through that with his family, and especially with Judy and all of us.

Q: If he got somebody else pregnant, and he was on drugs and alcohol, I can see where he might leave Judy, stay out of town, never see her again, whatever. Did you wonder why he didn't just do that, instead of doing what he did? The situation doesn't explain what he did.

A: I would ask myself why didn't he walk away, get a divorce, go on his merry way, and leave Judy and the children alone. That has always been my uppermost question.

Q: How did you handle feelings of that never being settled? How did you deal with that inside yourself?

A: I still have that frustration, that I really can't explain it. You know, you keep going back to "Did he love her, then did he change," and that kind of thing. And why, and how in the world, could he have gone to this length? These questions are just unanswered questions. I finally came to realize that I would never, ever have the answer to those questions.

94

Q: How long after it happened did it occur to you that you would never have those answers?

A: I guess it was several weeks, into the court hearings.

Q: In a certain way, did the realization that those answers would never come, help you to stop asking yourself that so much?

A: Yes, it did. That's when I had to just realize that it happened.

Q: That sounds to me like the beginning of really looking at the things we can't change.

A: That's right.

Q: But was there a part of you that said it's actually wrong to accept this kind of thing? Even if you're supposed to accept what you can't change?

A: The reason I was able to come to terms with it was that in reading a lot on death, anger, and grief, I came to see that if I didn't accept it, it would eat me alive and destroy my life. And I knew, too — especially while he was in jail and after he went on to prison for life — as I would think about it, I knew that my harboring this anger was not hurting him one bit.

Q: When you said to yourself, "I am beginning to accept what I cannot change, that this can never be changed," did you ever feel that it was wrong for Judy's memory to move into acceptance? Did you ever think that for Judy's sake you should not accept it?

A: No, not really. At different times I wondered to myself, let's say that if he had injured her but she had lived, I had to think that until that point, it would never have occurred to her that he could have even thought of something so brutal, much less done it. And so that helped me to not harbor that anger toward him, because that was how she would have felt.

Q: Because her love for him was so strong?

A: Very definitely. Oftentimes, when I would try to point things out to her, or talk to her about him, she would always come back, But Mother, he's my husband, I love him, he's my best friend. That's what she always said — he's my best friend. Well, you see, he wasn't. *She was his best friend, but he wasn't her best friend.*

Her daddy tried to explain that to her on occasion, but her love was just so deep for him, and she thought he was going to make changes, make things right, come back home.

Q: I think I'm hearing that even if she would have had to face the truth about him and divorce him, she would never have hated him.
A: No, she would not have.

Q: So that helped you to not hate him.
A: That's right, knowing how she felt, and how dedicated and committed to their marriage she was. And, along this line of anger, I realized when it came to Judy's children, that I had to be as much like her in caring for them as I could. I couldn't care for them and be there every day for them if I were saying ugly things about him, or thinking them, or talking. That would have influenced my life in the care of them. So I think my responsiblity to the children helped me.

Q: Even knowing all this, you still had to work through your feelings — you couldn't just go straight on to forgiveness. And that took a long time. The struggle was knowing where you wanted to be — and knowing where you were. Every time you went back to where you were — as opposed to where you wanted to be — I know you prayed, but what else did you do beside prayer to get on?
A: I reached out to others. I don't know what I would have done without family relationships, the support of family and friends who were here with me to talk with me and listen to me.

Q: They always encouraged you to keep talking your feelings through?
A: Yes.

Q: Did they always support you, no matter whether your feelings were forgiveness or anger? Did they support you wherever you were with your feelings at the time?
A: Yes, they really did.

Q: They weren't judgmental when you were angry, and when you felt forgiving, they didn't say, How can you forgive?
A: That's right. Some people would make the statement, "I'm glad you can forgive, but I can't. I'm happy that you can feel this

way, but I can't. I cannot forgive Russell, and I just have to harbor this feeling."

And then, too, I felt a responsibility to other people, to try to help them. Whenever I have given talks in churches or to civic groups, I always run into other people who have had crisis situations, and I find myself trying to encourage them. I think that's a big key — reaching out to other people who are going through something similar to what you yourself are going through.

Q: You know, that's very much like what happens when people are in recovery for alcoholism. In Alcoholics Anonymous, they are told that if they are going to stay sober, they have to reach out to help others. You're talking about the same thing. In your experience, to get to forgiveness yourself, you have to try to help other people who are also having trouble with forgiveness.

A: That's right. It is like that.

Q: Let me ask you this. As a minister's wife, at times when you were feeling still angry, did you feel some kind of pressure to act as if you were further along than you really were — to make those who know you think that you were doing as you believed you were supposed to do?

A: You probably could say that. I do believe people really expect you to behave in a certain way. But, in this situation, other people were so shocked and horrified that I don't think I had a lot of that put on me by others.

Q: Because it was so bad, they hardly expected anything of you?

A: That's right.

Q: What was your reaction when you spoke with him and he asked you to forgive him? Did you feel that you should, or shouldn't?

A: I found my answer in Scripture — Matthew 6:15. "If you do not forgive men, then your Father will not forgive your transgressions." I realized that in forgiving I was choosing obedience to the Lord, and the freedom that would bring.

Q: What was your reaction to the judge's sentence?

A: Many times after he was sent to prison for life, as opposed to getting the electric chair, lots of people would say to me, Aren't you disappointed? Don't you feel that he got off too light? I never have understood whether this is right or wrong for me to say this, but my thinking is that for him to sit in jail the rest of his life is far, far more punishment that being put to death instantly. If someone had pulled the switch and he had been gone, it would have been over with and put him out of his misery, and maybe we could have gotten to closure quicker, or something, I don't know. But I still say that for him to sit down there, he still has to think about this in some measure.

Q: When you began to forgive and find some peace inside yourself, did you sometimes think, "Oops, that's letting him off the hook when I'm not mad at him?"

A: Yes, I'm sure I did at times, because keeping a forgiving spirit is an ongoing process.

Q: People sometimes feel that somehow when you forgive someone, it's like letting them get away with it.

A: Nothing can bring her back — the hurt will always be there, and to think that he was responsible was hard to take, being a son-in-law and being in our home. I'm sure that any time a family member is involved with such a thing, it's harder for people to take and to accept. I forgave, but that does not change his guilt or punishment.

And then, I did have to think often, and I still do think of this today, the fact that Kelver, my husband, and I were supposed to have been killed too. That thought comes back, and I think about that, daily. Whenever I wake up, I thank God for that day, realizing that it might not have been. We came so close. And that is a different type of feeling towards him.

Q: How is it different?

A: To take Judy's life was one thing — the children's mother — but if we had gone, that would have been everything the children had, because Rusty was going to be gone too, in jail. And then, too, for our children, as much as for the grandchildren, it is hard to think about that. And so, for that reason, I would not let myself dwell on that. Really, I think somebody could go off mentally if they sat and brooded and thought about things like that. That could consume your life.

Q: About Judy's children — the oldest one was three when he found his mother. You said he was in therapy for about a year.

A: That's right.

Q: You know, a lot of people have children who have been traumatized. Can you talk about what kind of therapy helped him?

A: Everything was done through play therapy, letting him act out. That is their way of relieving the frustration that he would have had. He went five days a week for four weeks; then after that every other day; then it finally became two days a week; then one day a week, just tapering off, for about a year.

Q: So he went to a lot of sessions.

A: He did. And he loved to go. Of course he didn't know what it was for.

Q: How long was each session?

A: The therapist did that "by ear," depending on his needs that day. Never over an hour and a half, and most of the time more like 45 minutes.

Q: She was a child psychologist?

A: Yes. If he was tired, or if he was not reacting well, she would just cut it short. They videotaped every second of the sessions, and then each time after he left, she sat down with a group of psychologists and psychiatrists and they played it back, and that's how they decided what they were going to do the next session. They added some props and materials to their playroom, as they felt they were needed. Forrest was not verbalizing anything, but they said that they could observe from the way he used the therapeutic toys what he had seen, and get it out of his system.

Q: And they felt after that year that he had resolved a lot?

A: Oh, yes. I do think a lot of how much he has healed has to do with our starting the sessions with him immediately. You know, he started the very next day.

Q: On the very next day?

A: Yes. On that first morning, one of the detectives came to me and said, I need to speak to you privately, so we went off in the kitchen. And he said, I have Forrest's first mental-health session set for tomorrow at four o'clock. I was still in such shock, and I said, What did you say? And he said, Oh, Mrs. Mullins, in this situation this is mandatory. We have already set this up, and the Johnson City Police Department pays for the intake and the beginning session. So then I realized what he was saying, and of course I was floored that he had done this, because this had not crossed my mind. So then I just said, Oh, thank you!

Then, the next day, when his daddy and I took him —

Q: His *father* took him?
A: Yes, he went with me to take him. And Russell filled out all of the forms, so that his insurance would cover it.

Q: Oh, my.
A: Yes, at first, we all sat down together with several of the mental-health center staff, and the doctor in charge just observed Forrest to see what he was doing. Another man was sitting beside us that I knew to be an employee of the mental-health center, but I didn't know exactly who he was. After we had talked for just a minute, this man asked Forrest if he would like something to drink. Now I realize that he was wanting to get him out of the room so that we adults could talk, but I didn't know that then.

Forrest looked over at me and said, I will have to ask my MeMe. Because Judy never let him have something to drink before meals — you know, soft drinks. So I said, Yes, Forrest, it will be fine. Then the man asked, What would you like? and Forrest said, Well, chocolate milk is my favorite. And the man said, I don't believe we have any chocolate milk, but he told us everything that he did have, and Forrest said, Then I think I'll have a Pepsi. So Forrest got up, and the man sitting beside us got up and took Forrest's hand, and the two of them walked out of the room.

As soon as they closed the door, the fellow in charge nearly jumped up in the air and said, Oh, I don't think you have a thing to worry about! And of course, I said, What? And he said, We have just conducted our first experiment with Forrest. Usually for any child who has just gone through something like what Forrest has gone through, nine out of ten such children would not leave the room with a stranger. That doctor said the fact that Forrest would take this man's hand and leave the room with him told him a great deal.

Q: He was saying that Forrest's inner trust was not shattered?
A: That's right.

Q: Judy had given him one incredible beginning.
A: Yes, she had. And so they went off and stayed gone for a while, and the man took him to a play area, and got him something to drink and a cookie. Then, when they came back, the fellow thanked Forrest for coming to see him, and asked him if he would like to come back another day, and Forrest said, Yes I would! And he told him, Well, we want you to come down and see us. We've got some things for you to play with. So you see, they just won his love that day. And after that, every time I told him it was time for us to go, he was just ready. He loved it. They let him build things, they had a sandbox, and they would watch him build things and make things, and they would let him paint and draw.

Q: I wish that everybody whose children are traumatized could know the tremendous importance of getting the child in for help immediately, the very next day.
A: Yes, a lot of people might just think, "Well, it'll be all right."

Q: Or that he'll outgrow it or forget it. But those memories are stored unless you get them out.
A: The lady told him one day she would like for him to bring pictures, so that he could show her his family. So we came home and got pictures, and she just started right from the beginning with his mother, talking about her in good ways. One thing she had to deal with was that he told her one day that his mother wouldn't talk to him that morning, when he ran over to her. And so they had to work on that, to keep him from having anger toward his mama for leaving him.

Q: How did they do that?
A: Well, just by talking to him about her, and the fact that she didn't cause this, that someone else caused it. So that helped him to realize that it wasn't anything she did on purpose, to leave him.

From the beginning, while Forrest was going for his counseling, I had started to write down on paper all my own feelings and reactions to Judy's instant death. I wanted it to be some type of memorial for Forrest and Hunter to have about their mother, and I found that as I worked on it, it was very therapeutic for me.

This was when I began to tell the family that I was going to write a book. They all just sort of let me talk. I guess they all just thought, Well, just let her get that out of her system — she won't do it. So nobody told me not to, or that I couldn't, or anything like that. In fact, they really encouraged me.

Q: Did you also think you should do it to help other people?
A: I did. And so as I kept writing, I would always be thinking what I could say or do that someone else in a similar situation might find helpful, in the long run.

Now that the book is finished, I am very grateful to my publisher, Toby Rice Drews, of Recovery Communications, Inc., and to my editor, Betsy Tice White, for their encouragement and skill in helping this book become a reality.

It is my heartfelt tribute to Judy — a life remembered, a tragedy overcome.

Epilogue

A PRAYER FROM AFRICA,
A BIBLE FOR WORLD MISSIONS

ᥩ᭨   One of Judy's favorite people in all the world was my brother Webster Carroll, a missionary serving in East Africa for over 40 years. As soon as our children's "Uncle Web" heard of Judy's death, he flew immediately to Tennessee and stayed with us continually throughout the next week, offering wonderful consolation and strength to all. Traveling about afterward and using our place as home base, he came back to us again on the sorrowful day when we received news of Russell's arrest.

On the night before Webster finally flew back to Africa, he asked a favor of me. He had received a request from his wife Betty Lou, who had remained in Africa during our trouble. One of the African pastors, Pastor Isaac Ijalana, told Betty Lou he had been praying for a New American Standard Bible just like hers, which happened to have a dark burgundy cover. Caught up in the frenzied flurry of last-minute packing, Webster asked if I could go to a bookstore to purchase one. I assured him I would be happy to do so, in plenty of time before his flight.

After I told Kelver of Webster's request, he remarked that we had numerous Bibles downstairs in our own library and perhaps might give one to this deserving man. Right away we went downstairs to see. Unthinkingly, instead of going left into the library, I turned right into Judy's room, and there, on the night stand beside her bed, lay a dark burgundy Bible. Opening to the first page, I saw the words, "New American Standard Version."

Running into the library, I handed Kelver Judy's Bible, pointing to the title page. We both shed tears, and Kelver said, "Let's send it to this dear pastor in Africa." We prayed that Pastor Isaac could use it for his study, his growth in the Word, and his proclamation of its message to many who would come to accept Christ as their Savior — all of this through Judy's own, dark burgundy, New American Standard Version of the Bible.

The next morning we saw Webster off at the airport, and when we presented our treasure to him, all three of us wept together. I asked my brother to put an appropriate inscription in the front of the Bible before giving it to Pastor Isaac.

Three months after Judy's death, we received Webster's report:

Dear Kelver and Mattie,

It was a tender moment indeed when Pastor Isaac and Esther Ijalana came to our house and we presented him with Judy's Bible. They had already been so broken about her death and have really prayed for you all and the whole family. He read first what I had written inside:

In memory of Judy Mullins Freels, who, despite her tragic and untimely death at 31 years of age, sincerely walked with Jesus, and was a Godly mother and witness for her Lord.

Presented by Rev. and Mrs. Kelver Mullins, Judy's parents, praying for you to proclaim that same Jesus.

After Isaac had read these words about three times, placing his forefinger on each word as he read, he just glowed and said, "God has planned to do a mighty work in Africa with her life and her book."

Webster also sent us pictures taken as he gave the Bible to Brother Isaac and his wife Esther. *"They are overcome with awe and appreciation,"* he wrote, *"realizing that you had sent Judy's precious Bible. They are so grateful. I do not know of anyone who will use it more."*

A few weeks later we received another letter from Africa — a priceless one.

Dear Rev. and Mrs. Kelver Mullins,

Calvary greetings in the name of our Lord Jesus Christ. We are grateful unto God for you and for the comfort He bestowed on your family during the loss of your daughter, Judy Mullins Freels.

We learned of her death through Sister Betty Lou Carroll. Little did we know that her Best Book . . . . the Bible . . . . would become ours in our family. We accepted the gift made on her behalf by you through Rev. and Mrs. Webster Carroll, with deep love and appreciation.

I am a Nigerian by nationality, married to Esther, a Nigerian too, with four children: two girls and two boys . . . . We are missionaries in Uganda from the Deeper Christian Life

Ministry, with the headquarters in Lagos, Nigeria.
We hereby express our love to your family and your ministry.
The Bible was an answer to prayer. It was a precious gift. It has
opened my eyes to many hidden truths and difficult verses. We
pray that our warm love should be given to the children of Judy.
We shall be happy if her picture and those of her children could
be sent to us.
May the Lord continue to bless your home and ministry.

Yours faithfully
Isaac Ijalana

Here are portions of the letter I wrote to Pastor Isaac in return:

Your letter thrills us more than you will ever know, to
realize Judy's precious Bible has traveled over 2,000 miles from
the U.S.A. to East Africa intended for you, Brother Isaac, a
dedicated servant of the Lord . . . .
Judy was a precious, beautiful, and talented young woman,
dedicated to the Lord Jesus Christ . . . .
Our prayer is that God will richly bless you as you read,
study, and preach from this book, Judy's Bible. We will follow
your ministry as God continues to use you in winning many souls
to the saving knowledge of Jesus Christ . . . .
The Lord has certainly given us daily strength and guidance
in facing this tragedy in our lives. Already we can see how God
is using Judy's death to bring individuals to a closer walk with
the Lord . . . . Many have told us how their homes and family
situations have been given over completely to God and they have
dedicated themselves in a new way to the Lord's leadership in
their lives.

We can never forget how Judy longed to go as a missionary to a
foreign land, to spread the Gospel to the lost. Now confident that,
through her Bible, she is doing exactly that, I feel deeply satisfied.

THE JUDY MULLINS FREELS
MEMORIAL SCHOLARSHIP FUND

On September 29, 1995, just over a year after Judy's death, Carson-Newman College officially named the Judy Mullins Freels Scholarship. By that time hundreds of family members and friends had helped to make it possible, contributing more than $30,000 to the fund. All members of our family participated in the announcement ceremony. The fund continues to grow.

Recipients of the scholarship will be those who possibly could not otherwise receive an education — ministerial students or those involved in missions and music. "We hope and pray that through generations to come Judy's heritage will continue to live on," her father said at the dedication ceremony, "that it will be a blessing to others as long as time exists and this institution stands for the purpose of Christ."

Carson-Newman's President, Dr. Cordell Maddox, accepted the scholarship fund on behalf of the College and thanked the family for remembering Judy in such a fine way.

Proceeds from the sale of this book will be added to the scholarship fund. If you are interested in helping to support future generations of Christian young people in their education at Carson-Newman, you may do so by making your own contribution to the fund. For more information, call or write:

The Development Office
Carson-Newman College
CNC BOX 71993
Jefferson City, Tennessee 37760
Phone (423) 471-3232
FAX (423) 471-3502

Appendix

BECKY'S LETTER

Dear Forrest and Hunter,

I wanted to take a few moments to share with you a few of my memories of your mother, my sister, my best friend.

Some of my fondest childhood memories are of sharing a room together. We had deep-blue carpet in our room which we often referred to as "the water." I remember late at night when we would have to get up, we would throw our pillows down on the floor to make "the rocks," then jump on them from "rock" to "rock" all the way to the door as we went to the bathroom, so that the alligators would not get us as we crossed "the water." Oh, we used to giggle and screech as we cheered each other on across the dangerous waters! There are so many special things like that that we did, and I look forward to sharing more of those "when I was a little girl" stories with you in the future.

In middle school and high school, I recall the clubs we were in — NJROTC, Annual Staff, Civinettes, and, of course, Choir. Choir was our life. There were musicals, plays, and performances of all kinds. We were in every one and did everything. Your mom loved to sing and loved her music.

My first year at Carson-Newman was the first year she had not been my roommate. But we remedied that when she followed me the next year. We were about as close as sisters could be; however, no one could believe we would go off to college and be roomies.

The second year we lived apart was her senior year, while I lived in Africa. But then she graduated, and as soon as I returned, we were roommates again. I taught school in Newport, and she drove to Gatlinburg every day to work. We loved our little house. We did everything and went everywhere together.

When I moved to Knoxville to teach, Judy moved too. We lived together there about four months, until your mom was to marry. This is when I met Uncle Stephen. He was your dad Russell's roommate at Carson-Newman. So we even dated together.

What fun times we had as we began to have our families. Forrest and Hunter, you were the joy of her life. I so regret that my own boys will never know her and see the joy she had in her life. It is difficult as I try to explain things to them at times; however, my heart is also burdened that *you* will not know her, nor her you. I promise to help keep her memory alive for you, by sharing more stories in the years to come.

We did all suffer a shock, and I am convinced that it will take time for the healing to occur, but I claim Jeremiah 33:6: "Nevertheless, I will bring health and healing to it. I will heal my people and will let them enjoy abundant peace and security." Please *know* that our God continues to take care of us and provides for us. We can "give thanks to the Lord Almighty, for the Lord is good, and His love endures forever" (Jeremiah 33:11).

As you get older and have questions, may you know that He tells us, "If we call to the Lord, He will answer us and tell us great and unsearchable things we do not know." He can help us to understand these things, for He tells us, "'I know the plans I have for you,' declares the Lord, 'plans to prosper you and not harm you, plans to give you a hope and a future. Then you will call upon me and come and pray to me, and I will listen to you. You will seek me and find me when you seek me with all your heart'" (Jeremiah 29:11–13).

And that is what we must continue to do — seek our Lord, for He promises to help us through the next mile. I am so thankful to your Aunt Sanda and Uncle Shannon for their love and support through the years. In a time when we weren't sure what life would deal to us next, one certainty was our relationship with our Lord and that He would carry us through. That was not to be questioned.

Please *know* that we know your mother's heart and the path she chose to follow. And even though she is not here to walk with you each day, we pledge to you our love and support as we all continue to help you down the path she began with you. We pray that path will one day bring you to the saving knowledge of our Lord Jesus Christ, so that you will one day truly be strong, confident Christian men who know whom they believe. I pray you will be spiritual leaders of your own homes one day, leading your own families in such a way to bring them to the understanding of a personal relationship with the Father as well.

The Lord tells us, "He will give you a heart to know Him" (Jeremiah 24:7). That was your mother's daily desire — "to know the heart of Jesus." May you seek that same desire.

Much, much love,
Aunt Becky

SANDA'S LETTER

Dear Forrest and Hunter,

I miss your mom more than I can ever tell you. For thirty-one years, I considered her my "little sister" — a sister that I remember so well as we grew up together. MeMe let me help feed, bathe, dress, and hold her from the day they brought her home from the hospital. I loved her instantly. I remember carrying her around on my hip, even after she was too big for me to carry.

As we grew and she started to school, I thought I needed to protect her. I would sit with her on the bus and walk her to her classroom every day. As we got older, we talked and dreamed of owning a beauty shop together! She would do all the hair washing, cutting, styling, and perms, and I would answer the phone, make appointments, and take care of the shop. Well, as you know, we never did really do that. But she did get to cut your hair, Forrest, and she even gave the rest of us perms.

Your mom loved life. She was always full of happiness. Even when things didn't go exactly her way, she always found the good in every situation. When she went to Carson-Newman College, and I came back home to attend East Tennessee State University, she was disappointed that we wouldn't be together, but she took joy in being able to room with Aunt Becky. She enjoyed her college years so much!

Three years after she was married, she learned she was going to have a baby. This was especially wonderful news for me, because I was going to have a baby, too. We called each other every day to see how we were feeling, what the doctor had said, what names we had in mind, and all other kinds of "mom" things.

Her baby was due October 15 in Knoxville, mine October 16 in Johnson City. Since this would be my second baby and her first, I wondered if Papaw and MeMe would go to Knoxville to be with your mom. As I prayed for us both to have healthy babies, I also prayed that they wouldn't come at the same time, so we could both have Papaw and MeMe with us.

Well, the Lord took care of it for us. Selinda was born two weeks early, on October 1, and Forrest, you were born two weeks late, on November 1! It was during this time that your mom asked my husband and me if we would raise her children, if anything ever happened to her.

Three and a half years later, when she knew she was going to have another baby, she was the happiest mom in the world. We were all excited. In the middle of a January snowstorm, Hunter, you were born. MeMe called and said you were having breathing problems and were going to be transported to another hospital nearby. We all wanted to go to see you, but the roads were so bad that by the time we reached the first hospital, you were already on your way to the second. There they put you in Neonatal Intensive Care, where we couldn't see you. You were ten days old when we finally got to see and hold you. Your mom always wanted me to be happy, and she knew that seeing you would make me *very* happy.

When your mom died, my husband and I knew you both would be ours. We had promised your mom that we would love and take care of her children, if the need ever arose.

Forrest, I remember the first time you asked me if you could call me "Mom." I was both happy and sad — happy that you felt close enough to me to consider me as your Mom, and sad that my "little sister" wasn't here for you to call *her* Mom. I promised you that I would keep her memory alive for you, to the best of my ability.

I love the moments we now share, as we tell Hunter about "Momma Judy" and show him pictures of her. It's exciting to hear all the wonderful memories you have of her. I pray they will remain with you forever.

Dad and I pray daily that the Lord will make us the parents He wants us to be and you deserve. We pray that you will learn to seek Him first in everything you do in life. We pray that in everything we do, we will set a good example to you both, and to Sheree and Selinda. They are proud to call you their brothers, and we are proud to call you our sons.

I love you both dearly!
Momma Sanda

Raisin-Oatmeal Cookies
(Judy's Recipe)

1 cup packed brown sugar
½ cup granulated sugar
¾ cup shortening
1 egg
¼ cup water
1 teaspoon pure vanilla
1 cup all-purpose flour
1 teaspoon salt
1 teaspoon ground cinnamon
½ teaspoon ground cloves
½ teaspoon baking soda
3 cups rolled oats
1 cup raisins
1 cup chopped nuts

Preheat oven to 350°. In a large bowl, combine and mix the shortening, sugar, egg, water, and vanilla, until creamy. Stir in remaining ingredients.

Drop by rounded teaspoonfuls about 2 inches apart on greased cookie sheet. Bake about 12-15 minutes, until almost no indentation remains when touched. Immediately remove from the cookie sheet. Cool on racks. Makes about 60 cookies.

For variety, you may also add semi-sweet chocolate bits, mashed bananas, or flaked or shredded coconut.

Acknowledgments

Literally thousands of people have helped to make this book a reality and been there for us, helping our family to heal.

To every one who buys a copy of this book, thereby adding to the Judy Mullins Freels Scholarship Fund at Carson-Newman College, our whole family is grateful.

Especially I want to thank my husband Kelver, our three surviving children and their partners, and all the members of our extended family who have been such a blessing to me.

In addition, Kelver and I wish to express our heartfelt thanks to the following individuals and organizations:

All the law-enforcement and judicial authorities who helped us through our time of trial — all personnel at the Johnson City Police Department, Washington County Sheriff's Department, Tennessee Bureau of Investigation, Alabama Bureau of Investigation, and the First Judicial District Attorney General's Office, and Mr. David Crockett in particular;

The many hundreds of family members and friends whose support means everything;

The National Crimestoppers Program, the Pet Dairy Corporation, Carlson Travel Agency, the Tennessee Governor's Office, and the family and friends who unselfishly contributed to the reward money in assisting to solve the case;

The media, whose daily updates, support, and presence helped to move the unraveling of our daughter's murder at a much faster pace than might have happened otherwise;

Our many friends in the Baptist community and other denominations who provided the spiritual support to see us through the hardest time any family could imagine;

And, finally, the Faculty and Staff at Carson-Newman College for their unwavering encouragement and interest in seeing the memorial scholarship become a reality.

3 Excerpts From Mattie's New Book:
Preachers' Wives Tell All!
Country Stories and Country Recipes from Country Preachers' Wives

෮ ෮ ෮ One Sunday morning, I was with the church Youth Group planning a mission trip the pastor and I were to lead, when a 14-year-old suddenly came running into the classroom, all excited and out of breath.

"Mrs. Mullins! Oh, Mrs. Mullins!" he yelled. "You should ought to have been down in the housing projects last night! Oh, it was just awful! This man came home and found another man in his house, and they commenced to yelling, and screaming, and cutting one another! Oh, Mrs. Mullins, it was terrible!"

"Well, I am sorry," was the only answer I could muster.

He clasped his hands to his chest and calmly replied, "Oh, it's all right now. Them rescue squad men came and gave that man mouth-to-mouth consideration. Don't worry. Everything turned out all right."

෮ ෮ ෮ I once belonged to a small Missions Reading Group that met once a month, with each member always bringing a "covered dish" to share for our lunch. One of the ladies would review a new mission book, and lunch would follow.

One day eight of us ladies assembled, left our dishes in the kitchen, and went to a classroom for our meeting. When noon came, according to custom, we all went to the dining room to spread out our food. We uncovered our dishes to find, to our utter amazement — eight bowls of baked beans! After sharing a good laugh, we decided to send one of our number down the street to bring back hamburgers and fries. Never before or since have I had the opportunity to sample eight different varieties of baked beans!

Mattie Mullins is available to
speak to your church or
community group.

You can call Mattie at
(423) 926-7827

FAX to (423) 926-9933

e-mail her at
Kelmat@BNOC.net

or write to
Mattie Mullins
904 Millercrest Drive
Johnson City, TN 37604-4315

Recovery Communications, Inc.
Book Publishing & Author Promotions
Post Office Box 19910 • Baltimore, Maryland 21211, USA

Now available through your local bookstore!

Jennifer J. Richardson, M.S.W. *Diary of Abuse/Diary of Healing.* A young girl's secret journal recording two decades of abuse, with detailed healing therapy sessions. A very raw and extraordinary book. **Contact the author at: (404) 373-1837.**

Toby Rice Drews. *Getting Them Sober, Volume One — You Can Help!* Hundreds of ideas for sobriety and recovery. The million-seller endorsed by Melody Beattie, Dr. Norman Vincent Peale, and "Dear Abby." **Contact the author at: (410) 243-8352.**

Toby Rice Drews. *Getting Them Sober, Volume Four — Separation Decisions.* All about detachment and separation issues for families of alcoholics. Endorsed by Max Weisman, M.D., past president of the American Society of Addiction Medicine. **Contact the author at: (410) 243-8352.**

Betsy Tice White. *Turning Your Teen Around — How A Couple Helped Their Troubled Son While Keeping Their Marriage Alive and Well.* A doctor family's successful personal battle against teen-age drug use, with dozens of powerfully helpful tips for parents in pain. Endorsed by John Palmer, NBC News. **Contact the author at: (770) 590-7311.**

Betsy Tice White. *Mountain Folk, Mountain Food — Down-Home Wisdom, Plain Tales, and Recipe Secrets from Appalachia.* The joy of living as expressed in charming vignettes and mouth-watering regional foods! Endorsed by the host of the TV series "Great Country Inns" and by *Blue Ridge Country Magazine.* **Contact the author at: (770) 590-7311.**

Linda Meyer, Ph.D. *I See Myself Changing — Weekly Meditations and Recovery Journaling for Young Adults.* A life-affirming book for adolescents and young adults, endorsed by Robert Bulkeley, The Gilman School. **Contact the author at: (217) 367-8821.**

Joseph L. Buccilli, Ph.D. *Wise Stuff About Relationships.* A gem of a book for anyone in recovery; "an empowering spiritual workout." Endorsed by the vice president of the *Philadelphia Inquirer.* **Contact the author at: (609) 629-4441.**

John Pearson. *Eastern Shore Beckonings.* Marvelous trek back in time through charming villages and encounters with solid Chesapeake Bay folk. "Aches with affection" — the *Village Voice's* Washington correspondent. **Contact the author at: (410) 315-7940.**

Jerry Zeller. *The Shaman and Other Almost-Tall Tales.* Enchanting storytelling and grace-filled character sketches from an Episcopal archdeacon and former Emory University dean. **Contact the author at: (706) 692-5842.**

AND COMING SOON . . . .

David E. Bergesen. *Murder Crosses the Equator — A Father Jack Carthier Mystery.* Volcanic tale of suspense in a Latin-American setting, starring a clever missionary-priest detective.

Stacie Hagan and Charlie Palmgren. *The Chicken Conspiracy — Breaking the Cycle of Personal Stress and Organizational Mediocrity.* A liberating message from corporate trainers about successful personal, organizational, and global change.